IMPERIAL MEDIA

IMPERIAL MEDIA

COLONIAL NETWORKS AND INFORMATION TECHNOLOGIES IN THE BRITISH LITERARY IMAGINATION, 1857–1918

AARON WORTH

THE OHIO STATE UNIVERSITY PRESS
COLUMBUS

Library of Congress Cataloging-in-Publication Data
Worth, Aaron, author.
Imperial media : colonial networks and information technologies in the British literary
imagination, 1857–1918 / Aaron Worth.
pages cm
Includes bibliographical references and index.
ISBN 978-0-8142-1251-6 (cloth : alk. paper) — ISBN 0-8142-1251-4 (cloth : alk. paper) —
ISBN 978-0-8142-9355-3 (cd-rom) — ISBN 0-8142-9355-7 (cd-rom)
1. Literature and technology. 2. English literature—19th century—History and criticism.
3. Mass media and literature. 4. Information technology in literature. I. Title.
PR468.T4W67 2014
820.9'008—dc23

2013034228

Cover design by James A. Baumann
Type set in Adobe Minion Pro
Printed by Thomson-Shore, Inc.

∞ The paper used in this publication meets the minimum requirements of the American
National Standard for Information Sciences—Permanence of Paper for Printed Library
Materials. ANSI 29.48–1992.

9 8 7 6 5 4 3 2 1

CONTENTS

ॐ

ACKNOWLEDGMENTS

Portions of this book were initially presented as papers at the Victorian Literature and Culture seminar at Harvard University's Mahindra Humanities Center; at the Modern Language Association, Northeast Victorian Studies Association, and North American Victorian Studies Association conferences; and as part of the faculty lecture series at Boston University's College of General Studies. On each occasion I received valuable feedback. Individuals who read parts of *Imperial Media* and provided criticism, suggestions, and/or support include Richard Menke, Chris Keep, John Picker, John Plotz, Ivan Kreilkamp, Eugene Goodheart, Laura Quinney, Aviva Briefel, Michael Booth, Vanita Neelakanta, Gillian Pierce, Duncan Bell, and Rae Greiner, as well as several anonymous readers.

I am grateful to the editors of *Victorian Studies* and *Journal of Colonialism and Colonial History* for permission to reprint material originally appearing in those journals, and to Sandy Crooms, Malcolm Litchfield, Eugene O'Connor, and the entire staff at The Ohio State University Press for all their labors on *Imperial Media*.

My sincere thanks go as well to the many colleagues, friends, and family members, particularly my mother and sister, who provided support and encouragement along the way.

The book is dedicated to Michelle Worth and to Charlotte Worth, who entered the world while it was in press.

INTRODUCTION

⊂⊙⊃

Among the novels shortlisted for the Man Booker Prize in 2010 was Tom McCarthy's *C*, a self-proclaimed avant-gardist's foray into the realm of historical fiction. *C* follows the fortunes (to quote the book's jacket copy) "of Serge Carrefax, a man who—as his name suggests—surges into the electric modernity of the early twentieth century, transfixed by the technologies that will obliterate him."[1] As this précis might indicate, one of the novel's most noteworthy (and, to this reader at least, most attractive) elements is its sheer besottedness with late Victorian information technologies: among other things, it constitutes a scrupulously researched, even recherché, reconstruction of an extinct media ecology. In the novel's first fifty or so pages, McCarthy manages to introduce every iconic information technology of the Victorian period, including radio, telegraph, telephone, phonograph (in both cylinder- and disc-playing incarnations), and photograph, as well as a "Projecting Kinetoscope" (McCarthy, *C*, 45) and, later, the cinema proper (there are more recondite devices on offer as well, including "manometric flame and typesetting machines, phonautographs, rheotomes, [and] old hotel annunciators") (ibid., 35).[2] Moreover, Carrefax's personal history and the history of contemporaneous information technologies are (designedly) difficult to disentangle: born in 1898 to a father performing early radio experiments, he goes on to serve in World War I, ultimately perishing in 1922 in Egypt, while engaged in the

1

construction of a global communications network in the service of Britain's empire.

The present book is about the media which so decisively shaped the world inhabited by the Carrefaxes, both *père* and *fils* (the former, fortyish in the late 90s, would have witnessed firsthand the birth of the telephone, phonograph, and cinema as well as, of course, wireless telegraphy); more specifically, it is about the role such media played in helping Britons to conceptualize imperial systems during McCarthy's characters' lifetimes. Accordingly, its primary documentary evidence will take the form of fiction, chiefly novels, written during the late Victorian and (in the case of John Buchan) Modern periods. But I begin with—and mean to linger a moment upon—McCarthy's postmodern performance first of all because it strikes me as an unusually reflexive and erudite, but by no means unique, example of the present-day survival, and continued relevance, of characteristically Victorian topoi associated with media, and their relation to imperial systems in particular. To adduce one episode among many: recruited by his cryptographically obsessed godfather Widsun (a mysterious, darkly avuncular servant of empire who would not seem out of place in Kipling's *Kim*, or in a novel by Buchan or Erskine Childers), Serge is sent to Egypt to aid in the construction of the "Empire Wireless Chain," a prospective worldwide web centered in the Middle East, with a proposed "eight stations . . . each two thousand miles apart, relaying from here to every corner of the Empire" (ibid., 243). Upon arrival in Alexandria, however, his first task is to see to the state of the empire's landlines, by assessing the havoc wreaked by the natives upon "His Majesty's communication network" (ibid., 244) as it is presently embodied (its telegraphic and telephonic cables). Serge's arrival in Egypt coincides with the beginning of the end of British hegemony in the region, and in depicting the aftermath of years of native unrest leading to this moment of (nominal) independence, McCarthy foregrounds the violence done to communications systems, along with the symbolic resonances associated with such an assault. As Serge's superior, Major Ferguson, puts it:

> "After we deported [Egyptian nationalist Saad] Zaghlul, the Egyptians chose to vent their anger not just on our businesses and residencies, but also on telegraph wires, phone lines and the like. Even the poles sometimes: hacked them down with a real vengeance, like a tribe of Red Indians wreaking sacrilege against enemies' totem posts. Which they were, in a way."
>
> "How so?" asked Serge.
>
> "Way I see it," Ferguson said, picking up a salt biscuit from a bowl on his desk, "a phone box is sacred. No matter how shoddy, or in what obscure

and run-down district of which backwater it's in, it's still connected to a substation somewhere, which is connected to a central exchange, which itself forms one of many tributaries of a larger river that flows straight to the heart of London. Step into a box in Labban or Karmouz, and you're joined in holy trinity with every lane in Surrey, every gabled house in Gloucestershire." He slipped the biscuit into his mouth like a communion wafer, then continued: "You've been attached to us . . . to assess the impact of these acts of telecommunicative blasphemy." (ibid., 244)

Given the novel's high degree of historical erudition, it is curious that McCarthy does not have Ferguson mention the event that would have leapt immediately to the mind of any Briton at that time and in this context, namely, the destruction of British networks during the Indian Rebellion of 1857 (the Major substitutes "Red Indians" for East Indians, but it is the traumatic memory of the Mutiny that would really underlie any such musings). Nevertheless such episodes as this one bristle with Victorian and post-Victorian clichés about imperial media: the ostensibly disproportionate significance attached to native assaults on the imperial network (a theme which I explore in detail in the following chapter),[3] the metaphoric collapse of imperial communication with quasi-religious communion, and so on.

According to this criterion alone *C* is hardly unique, to be sure. To judge by the representations of empire to be found within many works of neo-Victorian fiction and film, and other contemporary revivifications of the nineteenth century, modern authors, and audiences, remain largely in thrall to the media-inflected conceptual templates created by the Victorians themselves. The reason McCarthy's novel particularly appeals to me as a way of framing my study stems from its imaginative reconstruction, late in the text, of a historical moment at which the links—conceptual as well as practical—between the British Empire and the information technologies with which it was associated first began to be *dis*sociated. Once installed at the Ministry of Communications in Cairo, Serge learns that the Empire Wireless project is, after numerous false starts, finally moving forward. Unfortunately—as the following exchange, shot through with anxious feelings of both imperial and technological inferiority, between Serge and his superior Macauley makes clear—the empire itself is not long for this world:

"So, finally [says Macauley]: the pylon at Abu Zabal is to be completed. It'll be switched on in May, they say. About eight years too late—eight years in which the nation that had radio before all others has slipped hopelessly behind. The French alone have high-powered transmitters in Beirut, Bamako and Tananarive; America has five times more foreign stations than

we have; even the Germans match us kilowatt for kilowatt worldwide. It's
an embarrassment. . . . Now Whitehall's worried the Dominions will start
distributing counterproductive content through the airwaves—which is
why they're setting up, back home, a national Broadcasting Corporation,
to pump a mix of propaganda, music and weather reports all around Britain and, eventually, to every corner of the Empire. Which, in turn, is why
they've realised that they'd better get the Abu Zabal pylon up and running,
and start working on the next one, and the next. . . ."

"Strange timing," Serge says.

"What's that?"

"That we start broadcasting central content Empire-wide just as we
lose our empire . . ."

"The irony is, as they say, striking," Macauley concurs.

"They should play dirges," Serge suggests. (ibid., 266–67)

The *synecdoches* at work here are equally striking, and indeed crucial to
the generation of the irony: McCarthy pointedly juxtaposes two events of
1922—the independence of Egypt (the backdrop, again, of Serge's experiences there) and the birth of the BBC—which only acquire retrospectively
the kind of representative significance with which he wishes to freight them.
Only, that is, from our twenty-first-century vantage point do they emerge
fully as embryonic, contrapuntal emblems of a postcolonial, media saturated
world—a world in which it is tempting to discern the migration of the older
imperialist impulse into information systems themselves. By dramatizing the
beginning of a process of decoupling between these two conceptual domains,
the novel shows how it becomes possible in the twentieth century for (among
other things) the idea of a quasi-autonomous *media empire* to supplant that
of a media-*inflected* and -lubricated empire.[4] But this is only to reinforce
how powerful and prolonged had been the multifarious, collective process
of conceptual *coupling* which took place in the decades before McCarthy's
imagined moment of dissolution. My purpose in this book is to illuminate
that process of coupling, as it registered within representative works of literature during those decades.

The period I consider—approximately the four decades before the end of
the First World War, with a particular focus on the late Victorian period—
would of course merit a substantial and eventful chapter in any conceivable
history of either European colonialism or modern communications technology. It was during these years that Britain reached its imperial climax; this
was the heyday of new imperialism with its attendant controversies, vicarious exhilarations, and anxieties of decline. It was also, as Richard Menke and

others have shown, a time of fluid, rapidly evolving media ecologies, certainly in the industrialized West.[5] Both of these spheres—colonial and technological—were thus in a state of flux, rapidly expanding and changing form, in reality as well as in the imagination. Moreover, Britain's empire and its media were enmeshed in a symbiotic relationship, as information technologies were (and, it might be argued, continue to be) indispensable to projects of colonial expansion and control—a relationship well understood by Britons, and amply documented in recent years by Daniel Headrick, the outstanding historian of technology and empire.[6] But how, I want to ask here, did this vital relationship register within imaginative writing of the period? In particular, how did media help to shape the ways in which British writers thought about empires, especially their own?

Two decades ago, in his pioneering study *The Imperial Archive: Knowledge and the Fantasy of Empire* (1993), Thomas Richards pointed to the importance of the burgeoning fetishization of information in the later nineteenth century within imperial fantasies of the period. Rightly seeing in the rapidly expanding colonial systems of the day a collective crisis of conceptual, as well as political, integration (though he did not put it this way), Richards looked to the Victorian "knowledge explosion" (Richards, *Imperial Archive*, 5) for something like a master trope used to impose a comforting unity upon the increasingly slippery idea of empire.[7] He found it in the figure of the archive—the collective imagination, crucially but not exclusively within works of fiction, of a vast, Borgesian compendium of knowledge serving to prop up the vulnerable fantasy of British colonial supremacy. Calling the archive "the central myth of the British Empire" (ibid., 57), and tracing its multifarious incarnations within novels of the late nineteenth and early twentieth centuries, Richards provided an early, and stimulating, model for how a work of literary criticism might engage the vitally important relationship between Victorian colonial and information systems.

In the years since the publication of Richards's study, a rich and extensive body of work has emerged within Victorian studies, transforming our understanding of the impact of information technologies upon nineteenth-century literary production.[8] Some scholars, for instance (Laura Otis is the exemplary figure here) have sought to demonstrate how the emergent metaphor of the communications "network" seeped across disciplinary boundaries in the nineteenth century. Other work has illuminated the effects of the new media environment upon the human sensorium, from Ivan Kreilkamp's phonographic reading of Conrad to John Picker's investigation of Victorian "soundscapes." The interplay of literary form and new media has been compellingly delineated in the work of Menke, among others.[9] But while such work has often generated valuable local insights regarding the relationship between technology and colonialism in literature, sustained explorations of the topic have not been forthcoming. "The imperial network" may have joined "the imperial archive" as a convenient critical commonplace, but recent studies of nineteenth-century information technologies have, by and large, kept the colonial world at the margins.[10]

Without question, however, this body of scholarship has greatly expanded and enriched our conception of the deep and complex relationship between new media and imaginative writing in the nineteenth century, arming us with a powerful and nuanced set of tools for investigating the ways in which technologies from the telegraph to the radio served as "things to think with."[11] Scholars are, accordingly, in a better position than ever before to grapple with the question of how the Victorians, and their immediate successors, used media to think about empire. The time is ripe to engage more deeply the role played by information technologies in shaping the imperial visions of writers in this period, since without these technologies, contemporary systems of colonial exploitation and influence often proved, literally, unthinkable. The figurations of empire one encounters in such works are, in other words, largely the imaginative progeny of a sustained, reciprocal, and by no means monolithic or mechanistic exchange between these two historically parallel, similarly fluid, and intimately interlinked conceptual domains.

My first chapter, "Imperial Cybernetics," explores the conceptualization of the British Raj as a distributed system, a vision heavily indebted to the same information networks that played such a vital role in its administration and control. Early in the 1850s, a colonial surgeon who had been experimenting with telegraphs received a Parliamentary directive to create a network in India. Before the decade was over, a complacent empire had been rocked by a native rebellion that began with sepoys slaying British telegraphers and ended with their being hanged by telegraph wires—at least anecdotally. The network thus came to possess immense symbolic as well as practical value in Victorian India, a value exploited to the full by contemporary journalists, historians, and novelists. But in the Indian fiction of Rudyard Kipling, I will show, the figure of the telegraph-smashing sepoy would undergo a sea change, from mutinous Luddite into the native telegraph and telephone operators who populate his work so densely. Kipling's conception of colonial India as a hybrid network both drew upon and helped to shape late-Victorian notions of the Indian as a passive channel to be colonized by English language and culture while remaining dispossessed of meaningful agency. The native information worker figuratively signals a limited integration into the imperial system, in which power and subjectivity nonetheless reside at its interstices rather than its channels. But elsewhere in Kipling this imaginary division proves an uneasy one, and British fantasies of a supremely tractable Indian body are significantly complicated in his fiction by a host of contrapuntal figures.

Chapter two, "Imperial Projections," argues for the crucial role played by information technologies in helping writers to conceptualize forms of colonial and imperial space and time during the later Victorian period. I will focus on a pair of bestselling novels written in 1886—Marie Corelli's *A Romance of Two Worlds* and H. Rider Haggard's *She*—which can both be described, if in the case of Corelli perhaps counterintuitively, as imperial romances which rely heavily upon contemporary developments in media history in articulating a range of responses to the colonial realities of the day. While Corelli's fantasies of the spiritual world are anything but overtly political, their core conceit of a telegraphic network projected throughout the universe is manifestly indebted to the new, global networks of Britain's empire. In its figuration of interplanetary spirit-travel by telegraph, it illuminates the role of technology in facilitating the vicarious pleasures of colonial expansion at the dawn of the age of high imperialism. Haggard's work, by contrast, tends to complicate contemporary narratives of imperialist exploration and conquest by figuring potential colonial territories as heavily inscribed spaces, charged with stored imperial histories—and energies—of their own. Nowhere, perhaps, is this tendency more brilliantly realized than in *She*—the novel that would lead Kipling, famously, to liken the author himself to a medium or channel of transmission.[12] With its echoes of the new inscriptive technologies of the 70s and 80s (particularly the emergent cinema), as well as older media of storage and preservation, *She* reminds the reader that the prospective colony is never really a mere blank space on the map, and mastery of space-oriented technologies is no guarantee of imperial longevity.

Chapter three, "Imperial Transmissions," continues the analysis of the relationship between media and imagined forms of imperial space and time begun in chapter two, but shifts ground to the last years of the Victorian period: the high-water mark of British expansion, but also the period that saw the appearance of Kipling's sober "Recessional." The fin-de-siècle writing of H. G. Wells—which includes not only his best-known scientific romances but also some of his first excursions into the realm of social criticism and prophesy—is here offered as a particularly rich and striking example of how technology could help Britons to think the often contradictory thought of imperialism at this especially fraught moment. I show how, in the imperial satires *The War of the Worlds* and *The First Men in the Moon,* Wells elaborated monitory parables that used technologies such as the telegraph and new wireless to construct an imperial chronotope associating territorial expansion with cultural extinction. Meanwhile, in his prophetic writing of the same period, Wells envisioned technologically saturated utopias premised upon the eradication of all difference. Wells's own conflicted, even contradictory, views on empire thus loom large in my analysis. His writing of this period well illustrates, I believe, how media, as prostheses of thought, helped not only to articulate the imperial anxieties and fantasies of the age but also to gloss over the ideological faultlines between them.

Chapter four, "Imperial Informatics," focuses on the similarly wide-ranging literary production of John Buchan, the novelist, propagandist, and statesman whom Gertrude Himmelfarb has called "The Last Victorian" (see Himmelfarb). No mere armchair advocate of British imperialism, Buchan was involved firsthand in the reality of colonial administration (beginning with his youthful membership in Lord Milner's South African "Kindergarten"), and would explore imperial themes in his writing throughout his life, in works of nonfiction as well as the adventure and spy novels for which he is best remembered (including *Prester John, The Thirty-Nine Steps, Greenmantle,* and *Mr Standfast,* among many others). In this chapter I contend that Buchan's thinking about the nature, mission, and future of British imperialism—a subject seen by some critics as the touchstone of his career—was profoundly shaped by his thinking about information. Considered as a conceptual entity with its own history, information was undergoing a process of significant evolution or transmutation during Buchan's lifetime; here, accordingly, I seek to trace the development of Buchan's own "informatics," in the sense of a theory or conception of information, from his early writings on colonial reconstruction to his spy novels featuring Richard Hannay, written during and immediately after World War I. I argue that Buchan, prominent in the creation and development of Britain's early information agencies (he was leader of the first Department of Information, and held other important positions), came to conceptualize information as an essentially Platonic force, capable of imposing order upon a modern world threatened with chaos—which for him largely meant the dissolution of the civilizing force represented by Britain's imperial system.

In sum, I believe that looking more closely at the relationship between media and empire in the nineteenth-century imagination can serve not only to flesh out an important yet underexplored topic in Victorian studies but also to complicate our ideas about the role of such technologies in serving as prostheses of thought during the period. I hope that the story I tell in the following chapters may play a part in framing future discussions on these topics.

CHAPTER ONE

IMPERIAL CYBERNETICS

I

In an early, comic scene from *Mangal Pandey: The Rising,* Bollywood's 2005 epic-melodrama of the 1857 "mutiny," a group of Indian men, pointedly seated amid a stand of hookahs (indices of "tradition"), express disbelief at a report of the "taelly garaffe" allegedly now "connect[ing] the entire country through wires." This new expression of "Company" power only becomes comprehensible to them when it is suggested that the "white men have mastered black magic"—perhaps employing, as one opines, "witch's hair" for wire. Later, when the rebellion has broken out, we learn from an anxious British officer that the natives have "torched the telegraph office"; in a short span of cinematic time, bemused ignorance of the technology has blossomed into a focused act of violence against it.[1] What is particularly striking about these moments in this product of modern Hindi cinema is, it seems to me, precisely their venerability as proairetic atoms in traditional, *British* narratives of the rebellion. Indeed, despite the ostensible reversal of values represented by the film—the Company is evil, the sepoys heroic—it conjures with a set of codes (a widow rescued from the pyre by a British officer, the momentous parade-ground standoff over the greased cartridges[2]) very like those to be found in classic histories by the likes of Kaye and Malleson.[3] In invoking the topos of Indian hostility to the British wire, construed as an innate suspicion or incomprehension finding release, in the bloody hour of mutiny, in the network's attempted destruction, the makers of *Mangal Pandey* are in fact rehearsing a similarly durable theme to be found in a host of nineteenth-century mutiny narratives, as the native assault on imperial communications systems serves as a seemingly indispensable component of numerous works of fiction, history, and memoir.[4]

The threat of the mutinous Indian is certainly present, too, in the world of Rudyard Kipling's fiction—erupting at least once (as I will show) in an Alamo-like attack on a telegraph office. But the picture is complicated somewhat by the concomitant proliferation in his work of a seemingly contrapuntal figure, an interesting foil to the figure of the telegraph-smashing sepoy, who reappears in a variety of incarnations—namely, the Indian information worker. In *The Naulahka* (1892), to choose one of seemingly numberless examples, the American protagonist, Nicholas Tarvin, enters a telegraph office in Rhatore—"a desecrated Mohammedan mosque" with wires streaming into its fractured dome. There he encounters a slumbering native operator who, once roused, is able to adopt a tone of faintly pitying superiority in addressing him (Tarvin being, as it happens, himself adept at signaling):

A sheeted figure lay on the floor. "It *takes* a dead man to run this place," exclaimed Tarvin, discovering the body. "Hallo, you! Get up there!"

The figure rose to its feet with grunts, cast away its covering, and disclosed a very sleepy native in a complete suit of dove-colored satin.

"Ho!" cried he.

"Yes," returned Tarvin, imperturbably. "You want to see me?"

"No; I want to send a telegram, if there's any electric fluid in this old tomb."

"Sir," said the native, affably, "you have come to right shop. I am telegraph-operator and postmaster-general of this state."

He seated himself in the decayed chair, opened a drawer of the table, and began to search for something.

"What you looking for, young man? Lost your connection with Calcutta?"

"Most gentlemen bring their own forms," he said with a distant note of reproach in his bland manner. "But here is form. Have you got pencil?"

"Oh, see here, don't let me strain this office. Hadn't you better go and lie down again? I'll tap the message off myself. What's your signal for Calcutta?"

"You, sir, not understanding this instrument."

"*Don't* I? You ought to see me milk the wires at election-time."

"This instrument require most judeecious handling, sir. You write message. I send. That is proper division of labour. Ha, ha!" (Kipling, *Nau-lahka*, 89–90)

The Indian signaler exudes proprietary entitlement, a sense of pride and importance in his position, and a good-natured air of condescension, along with (unsurprisingly from the author of "The White Man's Burden," with its recapitulationist premise)[5] an irrepressibly infantile nature: "'Denver is in the United States America,' said the native, looking up at Tarvin with childish glee in the sense of knowledge" (ibid., 91). Here, as throughout Kipling's India, the native has entered the network, not only having undergone a sea change from mutinous Luddite to docile telegraphist (though the former figure is, again, by no means extinct in his world), but, in this case at least, "gleefully" enacting an idealized colonial relationship, "looking up" at the sahib to whom he appears as a child and remarking, "You write message. I send. That is proper division of labour." The note of racial superiority is sounded in the signaler's "childish" performance, certainly; but the specificity of setting is crucial as well: in the language factory of the telegraph office we are shown a "division of labour" within English itself, a dual and unequal relation to the language, with the white man presented as origin and author, the Indian as conduit or channel. Yet while the episode is both comic in tone and—to the English or (Anglo-) American reader—ideologically reassuring, it is troubled by a faint but definite ground-note of the uncanny: the Indian operator is first encountered as a "sheeted figure," a "dead man" in an "old tomb" who proceeds to rise disconcertingly from his ambiguous repose. As I will show when I engage more fully with Kipling's Indian fiction, the figure of the networked native can be a profoundly unsettling figure indeed.

In what follows I want to look more closely at the imaginary relationship between India and the wire in nineteenth-century British writing—from the mutiny to Kipling—in the belief that this relationship, and the evolutionary path it traced, constitute eloquent evidence of the importance of information technologies to the conceptualization of central questions of British rule in the Raj. Very often, that is, fraught issues of power and subjectivity (British as well as Indian) could best, perhaps sometimes only, be formulated by transposing them onto the conceptual domain of communications technologies and networks. Moreover, in looking at the cognitive uses of the Indian network in Victorian writing I mean to shed light on what might be considered the flip side of a much better-known (now and, doubtless, then) narrative involving the conceptualization of the increasingly worldwide webs of nineteenth-century telecommunications—I mean the role played by information systems in helping to sustain fantasies of global racial unity, particularly of a kind which would repair the sundered bonds of Anglo-American brotherhood. These have already been thoroughly, and ably, explored: for instance, in her study of the emergent conceptual relationship between "racial alliance and postal networks" in the late nineteenth century, Katie-Louise Thomas shows how Conan Doyle's *A Study in Scarlet* (1888) both draws upon and contributes to a pervasive strain of thought by which technological systems came to be metaphorically transmuted into organic ones, the better to enable the transnational flow of imagined English "blood":

> Both [William] Cowper and [Andrew] Carnegie desire that blood brotherhood might transcend nation. For Cowper, nations are strangely liquid, and the oceans solid: a barrier that keeps the blood of nations from naturally amalgamating. But, Carnegie triumphantly declares, the development of communication technologies means that the nineteenth-century ocean has become a channel—a web of channels—that will actually facilitate the transnational mingling of kindred drops [Cowper's phrase]. . . . In other words, "kindred drops"—which . . . must always be Anglo-Saxon—can now correspond with each other through the veinlike "All Red Routes"— the postal routes and telegraph lines that spanned the globe. Through the medium of postal networks, blood, for Carnegie and other Victorian writers, flows swifter than water. (par. 2)

Such biologically indebted metaphors of sanguinary mingling worked well, indeed, when Britons wanted to imagine connections with blood kin— whether those kin were associated with the mother country by severed colonial bonds (Americans) or intact ones (Australians, Canadians, South Africans, etc.). But what happened to this fantasy when it came to conceptualizing the integration of alien subjects into the "Greater British" network?

The glaring mote, the perennial irritant, in the eye of fantasists of consanguineal empire was, of course, India. In his 1883 *The Expansion of England,* which helped to popularize the Dilkean concept of "Greater Britain," Sir John Seeley in fact carefully distinguished between *two* such entities, which he saw as both radically different in nature and fundamentally incompatible with each other: the "Colonial Empire" and the "Indian Empire" (Seeley, *Expansion,* 207).[6] The inhabitants of the former, he asserts,

> are of our own blood, a mere extension of the English nationality into new lands. If these lands were contiguous to England, it would seem a matter of course that the English population as it increases should occupy them, and evidently desirable that it should do so without a political separation. As they are not contiguous but remote, a certain difficulty arises, but it

is a difficulty which in these days of steam and electricity does not seem insurmountable. (213)

But matters quickly become more problematic when one turns to the East:

> Now you see that this argument rests entirely upon the community of blood between England and her colonies. It does not therefore apply to India. Two races could scarcely be more alien from each other than the English and the Hindus. . . . [India's] population has no tie of blood whatever with the population of England. . . . [W]hile the connection of England with her colonies is in the highest degree natural, her connection with India seems at first sight at least to be in the highest degree unnatural. There is no natural tie whatever between the two countries. No community of blood. . . . (ibid., 213–14)

Clearly Seeley could, by this time, confidently expect his audience to supply the necessary conceptual links underwriting a seemingly paradoxical proposition: namely, that the prosthetic extension (by means of "steam and electricity") of a "community of blood" could count as superlatively "natural." (This is shown by his use of enthymeme here, signaled by the breezily elisional "Now you see.")

What was especially troubling to Seeley, moreover, was the fact that liberal, enlightened Britain, finding itself compelled simultaneously to forge global connections with the English-settled "colonies" and with India, must of necessity grow a second, Janus face, succumbing to a kind of imperial schizophrenia:

> Thus the same nation which reaches one hand towards the future of the globe and assumes the position of mediator between Europe and the New World, stretches the other hand towards the remotest past, becomes an Asiatic conqueror, and usurps the succession of the Great Mogul. (ibid., 205)

Interestingly, three decades earlier, the author of an article on the progress and future of the electric telegraph had formulated the matter in strikingly similar terms. If in 1854 Seeley (then studying at Christ's College, Cambridge) had happened to pick up a copy of the *Quarterly Review*, he would have read that "the restless spirit of English engineers, having provided for the internal telegraphic communication of Great Britain and her principal dependencies, seems bent upon stretching out her lines to the East and to the West, so as ultimately to clasp the entire globe" ("The Electric Telegraph," 84). But while *technologically* the latter connection presented, if anything, far greater challenges (a transatlantic cable was indeed laid four years later, but gave up the ghost within the month),[7] it came packaged with a ready-made conceptual metaphor of egalitarian kinship and brotherhood: "Here it [the proposed cable] would lock in with the North American meshwork of wires, which hold themselves out like an open hand for the European grasp" (ibid., 84). By contrast (and the contrast could hardly be more stark):

> *Whilst England would thus grasp the West with one hand, her active children have plotted the seizure of the East with the other.* It is determined to pass a cable from Genoa to Corsica, and from thence to Sardinia. From the southernmost point of the latter island, Cape Spartivento, to the Gulf of Tunis, another cable can easily be carried. The direction thence (after giving off a coast branch to Algeria) will be along the African shore, by Tripoli to Alexandria, and eventually across Arabia, along the coasts of Persia and Beloochistan until it enters Scinde [*sic*], and finally joins the wire at Hydrabad. . . . (ibid., 85, emphasis added)

For this writer, as for Seeley (writing at the dawn of the age of high imperialism over a quarter-century later), the same trope of imperial ambidexterity symptomatizes a pervasive and fundamental problem of conceptual integration: extension of the metaphorically copulative hand (or, in the later examples discussed by Thomas, arterial web) to alien shores (and subjectivities) is, literally, unthinkable.

Nevertheless, as I hope to show in this chapter, when wrestling with this abiding conceptual quandary, no less than when fantasizing about global arterial networks, Britons relied heavily upon the metaphoric domain of communications technology. As a cognitive tool, indeed, the Victorian wire proved almost infinitely adaptable, suggesting imaginary solutions to problems associated with very different colonial contexts. In the following section, after a brief discussion of early accounts of telegraphic innovation and penetration in India, I will consider the symbolic role of the wire in narratives of the 1857 rebellion; in both cases perhaps the preeminent trope to be found is that of parallel, inimical intersubjective networks occupying the same territory. I will then turn to the fiction of Kipling, in which can be found, with striking frequency and in multiple guises, the figure of the native telegrapher, ostensible sign of the peaceable insertion of the native into the imperial system. However, this integration, as I will show, is a deeply fraught one.

II.

The Indian telegraph was born in India. That is, unlike (say) the networks that would overspread Africa later in the century, it was in a very real sense a "native" production—one meriting, in many historical accounts, its own origin myth (as it were), parallel to but distinct from the technology's "official" history, featuring such luminaries as Morse, Wheatstone, and Cooke. Its creator—the colonial Morse in this technological-historical narrative—was Dr. William Brooke O'Shaughnessy, a medical man and inventor of Irish origin who first began to experiment with telegraphs in India in the thirties.[8] His early experiments were thus contemporaneous with better-known breakthroughs taking place on either side of the Atlantic: in 1837, the year Wheatstone and Cooke patented their version of the telegraph, O'Shaughnessy succeeded in laying thirty miles of operational wire; Morse demonstrated his own model, to both the public and the US government, in 1838. But O'Shaughnessy's labors, however impressive, attracted little attention until the early fifties, when he was charged by James Ramsay, Lord Dalhousie (who had become governor-general of India in 1848) with networking the Raj[9]—in a bit of timing that would come to seem, from the British perspective, nothing short of providential before the decade was over:

> Aware of Lord Dalhousie's keenness to establish the telegraph in India, O'Shaughnessy asked his principal patron, H. H. Wilson, to bring his 1837 experiments to the attention of the court of directors [i.e. of the East India Company]. Dalhousie leapt at the offer of O'Shaughnessy's experience and in March 1850 authorized him to proceed with an experimental line. In 1852 he succeeded in establishing communication between Calcutta and Diamond Harbour, eighty miles distant, whereupon Dalhousie sent him to London to win the court of directors' approval for an all-India network. Upon his return, Dalhousie appointed him superintendent of electric telegraphs. Work commenced in November 1853. In spite of the lack of trained staff . . . the first telegram from Agra reached Calcutta, 800 miles away, on 24 March 1854. By the following February, Calcutta was linked to Agra, Bombay, Madras, and Attock on the north-west frontier, a remarkable technological feat involving the laying of over 3050 miles of wiring through jungles, across deserts, and over unbridged rivers. Soon after, O'Shaughnessy was to hear both Indians and Britons acknowledge the telegraph as a key factor in Britain's victory over the rebels of 1857. (Prior 1–2)

It was indeed during the 1857 rebellion that the wire, and its destruction, would emerge in the British imagination as perhaps the single most potent conceptual space for the imaginative formulation and expression of the (nearly inexpressible) prospect of an independent—and hostile—Indian subjectivity. But first I want briefly to delineate what might be termed the British semiotics of the Indian wire in the period just before the "mutiny," by looking synoptically at a trio of representative accounts published within a span of three years.

These texts—Edward Highton's *The Electric Telegraph: Its History and Progress* (1852), Laurence Turnbull's *The Electro-Magnetic Telegraph* (1853), and the already-mentioned *Quarterly* article "The Electric Telegraph" (1854)—all served to represent the Indian network to the British reading public while it was in the process of construction. Together they paint a collective picture of a triumph of Western engineering within supremely inhospitable conditions, a picture painted by the use of language that is not, to put it mildly, ideologically neutral. O'Shaughnessy himself is depicted (not inaccurately) as a kind of combination of engineer and *bricoleur* whose ingenuity was sorely taxed by the absence in India of vital materials for construction—crucially, wire itself (Highton praises O'Shaughnessy's "energy and perseverance" in developing a superior telegraphic system in the absence of "necessary materials") (Highton, *Electric Telegraph,* 152). From the beginning, then, India was represented as a hostile space inimical to the English network, and this formulation would prove an enduring one. The resourceful O'Shaughnessy employed "such materials as he could obtain in India at the time"—bamboo poles, for instance (ibid., 151). But the truly novel feature of his telegraphic system was the substitution of "an inch iron rod" for cable—in pointed contrast, as the *Quarterly* noted, to the "delicate harp-string" of the European wire ("The Electric Telegraph," 84). While born of practical necessity, this innovation was felicitously adaptable to a discourse that made use of a thoroughly unnuanced language of penetration and dominion; the iconography of British potency was well served by the image of a system of nearly indestructible rods, sunk directly into the soil of its imperial possession. These rods had practical advantages that simultaneously spoke of unequal power relations: they could be produced, as Turnbull tells us, by "one village forge" worked by "two coolies" (Turnbull, *Electro-Magnetic Telegraph,* 170). Indeed, apparently the labor of telegraph-building was itself a salubrious gift to the native, a goal or good in itself: "This all infusing [*sic*] enterprise has aroused the lethargic inhabitants of the tropical climate" (ibid., 169). In fact, the advantages of a networked India to the native population were potentially boundless, or so the *Quarterly* suggested in a paternalistic aside within a

Machiavellian celebration of the technology's "power" as an empire-builder: "When these two systems"—the telegraph and the railway that followed in its wake—"are completed, the real consolidation of England's power in the East will have commenced, and the countless resources of the Indian peninsula will be called forth for the benefit of the conquered as well as the conquering race" ("The Electric Telegraph," 84).

A favorite, and suggestive, topos in such celebrations is the rods' imperviousness to the manifold dangers of a savage land. Several accounts mention the threat posed to telegraph wires by India's climate, fauna, and human inhabitants, among which three classes very little distinction is typically made: "The importance of this discovery of the superiority of rods over wire will be fully appreciated in a country like India, where the lines must often run through a howling wilderness, tenanted by savage beasts, or more savage men" (Turnbull, *Electro-Magnetic Telegraph*, 170). The telegraphic line needed protection from "crows," "monkeys," and the "trampl[ing]" of "passengers, bullocks, buffaloes, and elephants" (ibid.). River cables had to be sheltered "from the grapnels of the heavy native boats which are constantly passing up and down" (ibid.), and "highly ingenious arrangements" were developed to guard against "the fearful discharges of atmospheric electricity which characterize thunder-storms in the vicinity of the tropics" (Highton, *Electric Telegraph*, 152). The constant in these accounts is a vision of India as a hostile topography to be conquered by Western "ingen[uity]." Commentators seemed to take particular pleasure in describing the invincible strength, and even exterminative powers, of the rods—the *Quarterly* boasts that "the weight of the heaviest monkey is not sufficient to injure them" ("The Electric Telegraph," 84), and more than one writer gleefully relates how, by channeling a lightning-strike, they killed "swarms of kites and crows" that had perched on them (Turnbull, *Electro-Magnetic Telegraph*, 170). Particularly interesting is the suggestion of hostile agency attributed to the colonial environment. The *Quarterly*'s writer, for one, employs frankly, if facetiously, militaristic tropes in describing the confrontation between India and the telegraph, noting that the former's "troops of monkeys" threaten to put the latter "*hors-de-combat*" ("The Electric Telegraph," 84). Turnbull, presciently, makes the suggestion of a strange autonomy on the part of the telegraphic system yet more explicit: "The lines must therefore protect themselves, and this is secured by the use of thick rods" (Turnbull, *Electro-Magnetic Telegraph*, 170). Half a decade before the mutiny, India is already at war with the nascent British network.

It was, however, with the rebellion that the wire truly came into its own as a technology not only for facilitating, even preserving, British rule in India but for imagining its very nature—and for focalizing Anglo-Indian antagonisms in symbolic form. Of course, in tracing its cognitive uses during and after the mutiny I do not mean to suggest that the telegraph was "only" of symbolic value to the English: there is no doubt "that the British possession of the telegraph played a vital role in defeating the sepoy uprisings" (Wilson, *Victorians,* 493). Colonel Edward Vibart even appended to his memoir of the rebellion a kind of monograph entitled "How the Electric Telegraph Saved India" (and the casting of the telegraph as a kind of autonomous actor or protagonist is significant, as I will presently discuss). The author of this work offers, in effect, a detailed historical narrative of a single act of telecommunication, to which he assigns world-historical importance. Besides its role in suppressing the mutiny, the telegraph also flashed the news of this suppression across the globe, in one of the first messages wired across the ocean: in the brief interval before the first transatlantic cable failed in 1858, it was able to announce, its laconic, euphemistic expression wonderfully suggesting the voice of supreme power: "GWALIOR INSURGENT ARMY BROKEN UP. ALL INDIA BECOMING TRANQUIL" (Standage, *Victorian Internet,* 153), thus ensuring a place for the rebellion in future histories of the technology.

Interestingly, the telegraph is in fact offered, along with the railway, in at least one canonical Victorian history as a putative cause of the rebellion. "[T]he hierarchy of India," assert Kaye and Malleson in their *History of the Indian Mutiny of 1857–8,* "were alarmed and offended" by British "innovations of moral progress," but also by the "inroads and encroachments of physical science":

> A privileged race of men, who had been held in veneration as the depositories of all human knowledge, were suddenly shown to be as feeble and impotent as babes and sucklings. It was no mere verbal demonstration; the arrogant self-assertion of the white man, which the Hindu priesthood could contradict or explain away. There were no means of contradicting or explaining away the railway cars . . . or the electric wires, which in a few minutes carried a message across the breadth of a whole province. . . . The prodigious triumphs over time and space achieved by these 'fire-carriages' and 'lightning-posts' put to shame the wisdom of the Brahmans. . . . (138–39)

In any event, the telegraph would, indeed, become a prominent target of attack during the rebellion; there is historical basis for its off-screen "torching" in *Mangal Pandey.* And just as in Tom McCarthy's depiction of a similar attack on the imperial network in early twentieth-century Egypt, the Indian destruction of the British wire was not merely inconveniencing but, "[f]rom a symbolic point of view" (McCarthy, *C*, 250), profoundly significant. To Britons, the attack on the network was construed as the infliction of an emasculating or castrating wound: "The Europeans listened to the shouting of slogans, the crackling of flames. . . . The Indians were crying out that they had 'broken the Electric Telegraph and overturned the British Rule, and boasting they had committed these atrocities in the name of religion'" (Wilson, *Victorians*, 205). "Breaking" the telegraph could be construed as an "atrocity," presumably, chiefly because of its great symbolic importance, as an emblem of potency and "Rule"; the two objects of attack are linked here by a parallel construction that seems to render them equivalent rather than merely sequential. Certainly British writers stressed native ignorance of the technology and its principles of operation, even as the Indians were bestially attacking it, reinforcing the sense of a symbolic, rather than a tactical, act: in one novel (to which I will shortly return) the mutineers' violence against the telegraph poles does only limited damage, since "the one thing these black rascals don't understand is the importance of cutting the telegraph wires" (Tracy, *Red Year*, 138).

Contrasted with the figure of the enraged, network-smashing native is a particularly interesting figure that recurs in such texts as well, namely, the youthful (British) martyr of the telegraph office at Delhi, allegedly slain at his post during the first wave of the rebellion. Flora Annie Steel, in her 1896 mutiny novel *On the Face of the Waters,* imagines this operator cut down in the act of signaling, in a tableau only partially mock-heroic:

> "They will come soon," said a young telegraph clerk cooly, as he stood by his instrument hoping for a welcome kling; sending, finally, that bulletin northward which ended with the reluctant admission, "we must shut up." Must indeed; seeing that some ruffians rushed in and sabered him, his hands still at the levers. (239)

The jingoistic novelist Louis Tracy, probably best remembered for his paradigmatic future-war fantasy of 1896, *The Final War,* handles the same episode with uncharacteristic understatement in his *The Red Year: A Story of the Indian Mutiny* (1907). After a (far more characteristic) catalogue of luridly painted outrages, "vile deeds" (45) and "unheard-of atrocities" (22) perpetrated by bloodthirsty "scum" and "rabble" (21–22) and dwelt upon in loving detail by the narrator,[10] Tracy gives an account that again notes the youth of this dual saint of empire and telecommunications, as well as the primitive nature of his equipment:

In the telegraph office a young signaler was sending a thrilling message to Umballa, Lahore, and the north.

"The sepoys have come in from Meerut," he announced with the slow tick of the earliest form of apparatus. "They are burning everything. Mr. Todd is dead, and, we hear, several Europeans. We must shut up."

That was his requiem. The startled operators of Umballa could obtain no further intelligence and the boy was slain at his post. (46)

The scene is deemed important enough to warrant a footnote documenting its historical accuracy, while also—in the manner of myth at its purest—offering an alternative, in fact contradictory, version equally well-supported by authority. (I will return to this shortly.) Such after-the-fact beatifications in fiction are based upon contemporary encomiums; Sir Herbert Edwardes, for one, praised the young signaler's imperial skill set: "Just look at the courage and sense of duty which made that little boy, with shot and cannon all around him, manipulate that message which I do not hesitate to say was the means of the salvation of the Punjaub [sic]" (Vibart, Sepoy Mutiny, 265).

Of course, this heroic "boy," like the rest of the mutiny's English victims, is in due course avenged, and fittingly, the wire is itself often cast as an instrument or agent of this vengeance, a kind of information-technological analogue to the cannon notoriously employed to blow apart mutineers. At times it seems a quasi-autonomous avenger itself, exacting a direct, physical retribution upon the rebellious Indian body. In a much-repeated anecdote, one Indian called the telegraph-wire "the string that had hanged him." This may have been figurative, but Tracy vividly literalizes the conceit, as he imagines the telegraph as the site of execution: "As one of [the sepoys] said, looking up at a damaged pole"—damaged, that is, by the sepoys in their rampage—"which was about to serve as his gallows: 'Ah, you are able to hang me now because that cursed wire strangled us all in our sleep.' His metaphor was correct enough" (Tracy, Red Year, 258). This is only a particularly bloodthirsty depiction of the network as a seemingly living, volitional agent of imperial retribution; the wire that "saved India" has become a "metaphor[ical]"—indeed, as here, precisely more than metaphorical—agent of corporeal discipline and punishment. In this fantasy the network itself, the figure of English intersubjectivity, becomes capable of direct vengeance against the mutinous Indian.

It is, indeed, difficult to read accounts of the imperial wire, particularly those written during and after the mutiny, without concluding that the Indian network did function as just such a figure—as a trope, that is, for British subjectivity in the alien colony of India (or rather, the intersubjective structure which served as its condition of possibility) imagined as a prosthesis, technologically enhanced and mapped over colonial space.

In large part, no doubt, the figuration of what one might term a cybernetic subjectivity—a partnership of mind and wire—springs from (and resonates with) the perception of the British presence in India as an artificial hybrid. (Paul Scott's *Raj Quartet* is only one example of a fictional work that strikingly conveys the sense of the English social order as a rigidly unnatural transplant in India.) The sense of a transported or artificial English social network both modeled and precariously maintained by its technological analogues is well conveyed in Kipling's story "At the End of the Passage," with its depiction of four Anglo-Indians who gather weekly, ostensibly for recreation but more fundamentally, it is clear, for the purpose of mutually affirming a sense of their English identity. Professionally, these Britons are paradigms of colonial service, imperial men representative to an almost Chaucerian degree—their little society comprises an engineer, a civil servant, a colonial surveyor, and a "doctor of the line," a neat microcosm. While bound by little in the way of affective ties—"they were not conscious of any special regard for each other"—nonetheless "they desired ardently to meet, as men without water desire to drink" (Kipling, *Life's Handicap*, 139). As Benita Parry notes, the men's weekly communions are symbolic of a desperate, even obsessive Anglo-Indian circling of the sociocultural wagons within an "environment which disturbed and discomposed because it seemed to threaten their identity and values" (*Delusions and Discoveries*, 209). Kipling, significantly, portrays this quasi-ritualistic (re)instantiation of British colonial identity, this transplanted microcosm, as utterly dependent upon the networks of "the Great Indian Empire" (*Life's Handicap*, 148). The wire, frequently invoked within the story, binds together the four men within an alien, literally fatal climate:

> When one of them failed to appear, he [Hummil, the engineer and host of the gatherings] would send a telegram to his last address, in order that he might know whether the defaulter were dead or alive. There are very many places in the East where it is not good or kind to let your acquaintances drop out of sight even for one short week. (ibid., 139)

The maintenance of British identity in the colonies, then, seems impossible, perhaps unthinkable, without the prosthetic intersubjectivity upon which it is erected.

To us, of course, the identification or collapse of information systems with intersubjective networks has become something of a critical commonplace: speaking from (and for) a Lacanian perspective, for instance, Slavoj Žižek has aligned such telecommunications systems as the telephonic network in Anton Litvak's *Sorry, Wrong Number*[11] and the virtual reality construct in *The Matrix*[12] with the symbolic order, alias the inscrutable, transpersonal "big Other," maker of subjects.[13] Certainly some such reading would seem to illuminate the ostensibly disproportionate importance with which the telegraphic network is invested in the collectively constructed mutiny ur-narrative. The machinic or cybernetic symbolic order discernible in so many Anglo-Indian texts should, on such a reading, be taken to represent the "Other" of empire itself, understood as a seemingly autonomous, transpersonal entity whose address is necessary for the constitution of the Anglo-Indian subject. The sense of the telegraphic network as the privileged site for contact or communion with this imperial Other is strikingly captured by Steel: "An hour or two later, the strangest telegram that ever came as sole warning to an Empire that its very foundation was attacked, left Meerut for Agre; sent by the postmaster's niece" (*On the Face of the Waters*, 189–90). (Such an entity also looms large in Kipling's work, as I will show presently.) Moreover, on this view, the slain English operator, cut down in the flower of youth, ought to be understood as not just a brave British lad but a figure to be placed alongside such other conflict-specific archetypes as the soldier, the besieged Englishwoman, and so on. He represents youthful imperial subjectivity itself, positioned at the network's interstices and in privileged communion with Empire, and is its martyr, meeting his end in the irruption of the wire's own "Real," namely, its destruction by the constitutive kernel of its discourse; its central, ultimately perhaps sole referent: "MUTINY."

Also suggestive in this context is the tendency of many British accounts of Indian discontent to imagine not only, or even primarily, a putatively traditionalist or Luddite fear of technology, modernity, or innovation as such, but rather a coded or symbolic attack on British subjectivity itself. Of course, Victorian (as well as post-Victorian) narratives often attempt to construe the rebellion as, precisely, a symbolic war—not in the sense, of course, that it wasn't violently "real" (and beyond the sense that it "stood for" more than itself in the annals of Empire—it was "the epic of the race," and so on[14]), but in the sense that it arose from conflicts enacted in a symbolic register. This might help to explain, for instance, the focus on Indian fear of expulsion from a native symbolic order (through the consumption of proscribed foods) as the primary or even sole cause of mutiny, to the exclusion of other motives documented by later historians. In some versions, the rebellion is, one might say, reducible to the dissemination of a single datum or bit of information, a supremely consequential, yet purely symbolic, either-or: the knowledge that what a Hindu has tasted is beef, a Muslim pork.

In any case, mention of a "native symbolic order" leads us to the highly significant fact that the Anglo-Indian intersubjective network possesses, inevitably, an uncanny rival in British accounts. The same mutiny narratives, that is, in which the British networks feature so prominently usually provide a symbolic foil or counterpoint in the form of native systems of communication, media and practices either likened to or contrasted with (but in either case sharing a metaphoric ground with) Western technologies, to which the Indian networks are somehow both irreducibly alien yet strangely akin. While resistant to the incursion of British cables, India is in fact depicted as a space inherently conducive to the promiscuous flow of information: "In India," declares one writer, "news travels with a mysterious and miraculous rapidity" (Knollys, *Incidents in the Sepoy War,* 17). Its chronotope seems naturally susceptible to the swift, uncontrollable diffusion of messages, disseminated via tongues, bodies, and (other) conspicuously material signs, with a speed and reach rivaling or surpassing those of the telegraph itself.

In the first chapter of Steel's *On the Face of the Waters,* in which Steel uses the conceit of an auctioneer's cry of "Going! Going! Gone!" to suggest the unwelcome transformations wrought upon traditional Indian society by British rule, a narrative voice meant to represent a collective Indian consciousness expresses a disbelieving consternation like that depicted in *Mangal Pandey,* meditating upon "tales" "of news flashed faster by wires than any, even the gods themselves, could flash it" (Steel, *On the Face of the Waters,* 11). "Wires" are better transmitters than "the gods," but the very analogy implies a ground for comparison: the difference seems one of degree rather than kind. Later, Steel imagines the native intelligence network as an uncontrolled, parasitic extension of the telegraph, as one character complains: "The telegram is all through the bazaar by now. You can't help it if you employ natives" (ibid., 158). Often, as in Tracy's *The Red Year,* native networks possess powers either implicitly rivaling the telegraph's speed—"The lie [i.e. the supposedly false report of the greased cartridges] and the message flew through India with the inconceivable speed with which such ill tidings always travels [*sic*] in that country" (Tracy, *Red Year,* 2)—or explicitly besting it: "No man knows how rumor travels here . . . it beats the telegraph at times" (ibid., 131). The sense of a war between networks, preceding and prefiguring the more literal conflict, the familiar progression of set-pieces from Meerut to Cawnpore and Lucknow, could hardly be clearer.

Again, and unsurprisingly, there are essential differences between the two antagonistic networks, differences strongly delineated within these texts (and whose nature and significance I will want to explore further in my discussion of Kipling). This alterity is perhaps most clearly suggested in another oft-included component of the classic mutiny narrative, namely, the "mysterious" episode of the chapatis, one reproduced with striking consistency, from novels like Steel's to historical accounts like T. Rice Holmes's:

> [T]he English . . . were asking each other what could be the meaning of a mysterious phenomenon which had startled them a few weeks before. In January a strange symbol, the flat cake or chapatty which forms the staple food of the Indian people, began to pass from village to village through the length and breadth of the North-Western Provinces, like the fiery cross that summoned the clansmen of Roderick to battle. . . . The meaning of the portent has never been positively discovered. . . . (*History of the Indian Mutiny*, 90)

Henry Knollys's account in his *Incidents in the Sepoy War* is similar:

> In the middle of 1856 numerous villages in the north-western provinces were visited by messengers, coming no man knew whence, and conveying a mysterious token in the shape of chupatties . . . month after month this process was continued with inconceivable rapidity and secrecy, until at last every station had been communicated with. (Knollys, *Incidents*, 13–14)

Again—inevitably—"mysterious," but (or rather, consequently) necessarily a threat to British power; as Disraeli proclaimed in Parliament: "This is a secret communication, and therefore a communication dangerous to the government" (ibid., 15). While then rivaling, perhaps mirroring, the telegraph in many respects, in contradistinction to it native systems are characterized by a certain semantic ambiguity or polysemy, as well as a conspicuous grounding in the resolutely material sign—whether the body, the voice, or the cake of bread charged with "mysterious" meaning. (A similarly dualist conception would, as I hope presently to show, strongly inform Kipling's writing as well.)

As I have already hinted, the episode of the martyred telegraph-boy seems to have been mythic, not only in the sense of bearing a larger cultural significance but also in the simple sense of being untrue. This at least is the contention of the author of "How the Electric Telegraph Saved India," who certainly cannot be accused of a lack of investment or immersion in his chosen subject. Seeking to deconstruct the myth (thus showing, of course, that it had indeed attained the *status* of imperial myth, at least a minor one) he notes rather contemptuously of one history:

The writer goes on to say that the mutineers burst in on the devoted lad, the last click died away, and in the performance of his duty the signaller was slain. A touching and exciting story, but unfortunately (?) [*sic*] not quite true, as the signaller in question is still alive, and able to recollect what really did happen . . . . (Vibart 251–52)[15]

Whether the episode is literally true or not, the English boy who meets his demise in the colonial telegraph office was a figure that clearly fired the imagination of many British novelists and historians.

A half-century and more of mutiny narratives, then, circled persistently about the trope of the imperial wire, as the telegraphic network assumed its highly charged status as a kind of externalization of English authority. From this conceptual crucible, two archetypes in particular emerged: on the one hand, the murderous native Luddite, striking directly against Britain's symbolic network; on the other, the young English signaler, sending word of the rebellion to that network itself, with a courage and alacrity that led some to call him, without hyperbole, the savior of the empire. I want now to turn to Kipling, who blended aspects of both of these figures in his conceptualization of a character type that populates his fiction with great frequency.

III.

In *Rujub the Juggler* (1893), a mutiny novel for children (less well-known than the same author's *In Times of Peril*), G. A. Henty constructs a fantasy in which the loyal native not only remains faithful to the British cause but also aids it in the role of information worker: the novel centers upon the conversion, in essence, of a pair of natives into instruments of telecommunication for the use of their English masters. The "juggler" of the title first appears in his capacity as mere entertainer, performing a trick involving the mysterious extension of a "bit sawn off a telegraph pole" (Henty, *Rujub the Juggler*, 18), from which magically elongated perch his daughter then vanishes. This particular conjuring act is a suggestive one, since this pair possess, as it turns out, telepathic powers, together forming a circuit which the British heroes are able to exploit after the outbreak of mutiny.[16] In effect, Rujub and his daughter *become* the telegraph.[17] Rujub speaks of an elite class of "masters, who have powers that have been handed down from father to son for thousands of years, who can communicate with each other though separated by the length of India" (ibid., 279).[18] In the service of Henty's Britons, these native signalers are put to work in the service of Empire, allowing messages to be sent to an imprisoned Englishwoman, while also acquiring intelligence about the prison itself: as Rujub announces, "The information is of use, sahib" (ibid., 335).

The trope of the potentially mutinous Indian rendered useful to the imperium as a channel or medium of British communication—far from uncommon in the decades following the rebellion—deserves closer attention. In Henty's hands, to be sure, the figure serves as an ingredient in a relatively uncomplicated fantasy of native loyalty. But the prevalence, and manifold elaboration, of the trope also suggests a culturally broader attempt to engage imaginatively with the kinds of issues of integration—political and social as well as conceptual—relative to colonial India with which figures like Seeley were, again, grappling in the later nineteenth century. It is my contention here that the incomparably richer fiction of Kipling (richer, I mean, than Henty's) provides a particularly clear window through which one may view such efforts, and in so doing, to understand better the role played by information technology in helping British writers to conceptualize the integration of the post-mutiny Indian into the imperial network.

It is no secret, of course, that modern technology occupied a central place in Kipling's writing. A large portion of his life's work can justly be placed under the rubric of, in Herb Sussman's apt phrase, "The Romance of the Machine."[19] The feats and products of nineteenth-century Western invention figure prominently in his writing, from tales relating heroic projects of engineering ("The Bridge-Builders"), to stories centered upon a particular technology ("The Ship that Found Herself"), to full-blown science fiction featuring, for example, a fleet of airships ("With the Night Mail"). And information technology in particular provided a keen spur to Kipling's imagination, from his poetic exploration of submarine communications in "The Deep-Sea Cables" to his potently spooky tale of the new radio, "Wireless." Above all, the wire of the electric telegraph is woven inextricably into the fabric of his fictional world. Throughout his tales, not only are telegrams constantly in evidence, and often of crucial importance, but the reader is frequently led into telegraph offices (as well as newspaper offices that are depicted as termini for masses of chattering wire). Kipling's work, furthermore, demonstrates a fascination with the telegraph map as an imaginary representation of India as a colonized, administered unity; it is, indeed, perhaps one of the defining images of India in his fiction. Telegraphy also serves, as it did for many others, as a metaphoric ground for human communication more generally, as in "An Habitation Enforced," a tale in which a cosmopolitan American couple—the husband being sufficiently addicted to telegraphic communication as to have the estate they purchase connected by wire—seem irretrievably alien to the natives of the remote English village where they find themselves, natives whose gossip Kipling calls "farm-telegraphy, which is older but swifter than Marconi's" (*Actions and Reactions*, 22).

Furthermore, as even a fairly casual reading of his Indian fiction shows, Kipling had a particular fascination, amounting almost to obsession, with the figure of the native signaler—the replacement, as it were, of the martyred English boy within the telegraph offices of the sprawling web of empire. This figure appears, in multiple guises, seemingly everywhere in Kipling's tales of the Raj. I have already mentioned one incarnation, from *The Naulahka*. In some tales the Indian information worker plays a minor role, functioning more or less as part of the scenery. For example, in "The Daughter of the Regiment," an Irish private relates to the story's narrator, in heavily accented tones, a tale of a cholera-stricken "throop-thrain" wiring ahead for assistance:

> The Orficer Commandin' sent a telegrapt up the line, three hundher' mile up, askin' for help. Faith, we wanted ut, for ivry sowl av the followers ran for the dear life as soon as the thrain stopped, an' by the time that telegrapt was writ, there wasn't a naygur in the station exceptin' the telegrapt-clerk—an' he only bekase he was held down to his chair by the scruff av his sneakin' black neck. (Kipling, *Plain Tales*, 152)

(This cowardly figure is, in fact, unusual in having to be forcibly "held down" to his post; the "glee[ful]" signaler from *The Naulahka* is more representative.) Other examples include the "Madrassee telegraph-clerk" in "William the Conquerer" and the telegraph operator in "The Arrest of Lieutenant Golightly." Elsewhere the operator plays a more central, even pivotal role, as is the case with Gunga Dass, the treacherous telegraph-master in "The Strange Ride of Morrowbie Jukes" and Michele D'Cruze, the "shambl[ing]" protagonist of "His Chance in Life," respectively employed as "a Telegraph Signaller on Rs.35 a month" (ibid., 60).

In what follows I propose to consider a few of the multifarious avatars of the figure of the Indian telegrapher featured in Kipling's tales, in order to trace some of the ways in which British figurations of the imperial system in post-Mutiny India could be conceptually shaped by the wire.[20] Most obviously, the figure of the native information worker suggests the peaceable integration of the Indian into the imperial network; more, as a peculiarly forceful example of a native colonized, body and soul, by the English language, he symbolizes the Anglicized Indian envisioned by men like Macaulay, earlier in the century. In Kipling, however, the case is more complicated than this. As I will show, his fiction not only exposes anxieties associated with the prospect of a racially hybrid language network; it also, and more fundamentally, depicts the imperial system as a sublimely indifferent Other, in a fashion that tends to undermine the very hierarchies of nature on which British rule supposedly depends.

The Indian telegrapher from *The Naulahka* is, again, described as "childish" (91). Indeed, and unsurprisingly, the native operator, like other Indian characters, is often infantilized in Kipling. What strikes me as worthy of further consideration, however, is the persistent way in which this infantilization, particularly though not exclusively in the case of the signaler, also registers as a relationship to the English language itself. In his depiction of the Indian's relationship to English, I want to suggest, Kipling posits or imagines the presence of an essential and hierarchized division within language, one strikingly similar to that which Kristeva would identify as "*two modalities of* . . . the same signifying process" (*Revolution,* 23–24, emphasis original). I refer of course to her "fundamental categorical distinction between the semiotic and the symbolic" (Beardsworth, *Julia Kristeva,* 39), between on the one hand a modality associated broadly with the materiality of the sign (as well as, perhaps, revolutionary or anarchic connotations), and on the other the supposedly masculine domain of structured meaning and syntax (allied with law and order).

In fact, a powerful and pervasive association of the Indian with the semiotic (in, again, something very like Kristeva's sense) can be found quite early in the young writer's development: in a letter written from the press room of one of the Indian papers where he cut his teeth, the twenty-three-year-old Kipling, while sitting and "wait[ing] for the last telegrams," complains: "It isn't a cool night by any means and there is a mixed flavor of printers [*sic*] ink, baled paper, deodar wood and hot coolie that is not sweet" (Pinney, *Letters of Rudyard Kipling,* 173). This olfactory conflation, part of a larger mise-en-scène also comprising sleeping Indian boys and "native" workers whose drowsiness causes them "to mangle the wisdom of Reuter" (ibid.), renders vividly palpable the material conditions of linguistic production. And in linking the body of the "coolie," an ineluctable but problematic component, with such other textual ingredients as paper and ink, the young writer is establishing the formula that can be found throughout his Indian fiction—as, for instance, when Kipling displays native communications systems in all their material concreteness. There are, to take a pair of examples, the "object-letters" mentioned in "Beyond the Pale" ("Next morning . . . an old woman threw a packet into his dogcart. In the packet was the half of a broken glass-bangle, one flower of the blood-red dhak, a pinch of bhusa or cattle-food, and eleven cardamoms" [*Plain Tales,* 128]), and the "string-talk letter" in "The Man Who Would be

King" ("I remembered that there had once come to the office a blind man with a knotted twig and a piece of string which he wound round the twig according to some cipher of his own" [264]). In their inveterate materiality such systems resemble the chapatis inevitably, and nervously, invoked in British accounts of mutiny. Even integrated into the imperial information network as signaler, the native retains a decided association with the brute stuff of language,[21] in marked contrast to the disembodied flashes of telegraphic information, apparently (as we will see presently) the empire's own characteristic voice. He is, or is supposed to be, a passive channel for the messages that traverse his body as meaningless units (as the Saussurean arbitrariness of Morse, or—to anticipate an example I shall discuss presently—as fragmented, phonemic pulses issuing from the mouth), rather than an active producer of meaning. Or, to recall the words of the unnamed signaler from *The Naulahka:* "You write message. I send. That is proper division of labour."

This is not to say that the native signaler, the grounding body as it were for the imperial symbolic order, is always docile or trustworthy. Take the case of the dastardly Gunga Dass, the former telegraph master in "The Strange Ride of Morrowbie Jukes." When he first appears to Jukes, who had known him in his former capacity, he is terribly altered, decoded—"Caste-mark, stomach, slate-coloured continuations, and unctuous speech were all gone" (ibid., 8)—but Jukes manages to recognize him by a scar, and recalls what had been Dass's most memorable, if not defining, characteristic:

> He was in charge of a branch telegraph-office there, and when I had last met him was a jovial, full-stomached, portly Government servant with a marvellous capacity for making bad puns in English—a peculiarity which made me remember him long after I had forgotten his services to me in his official capacity. It is seldom that a Hindu makes English puns. (ibid.)

Zohreh T. Sullivan points to this trait, among other qualities, in noting Dass's "mastery over language," an "inversion" terrifying to the Englishman (*Narratives of Empire*, 75–76). It may thus be said that the former telegraph-master, destined to become a traitor to his own "masters," stands in an active relation to the English tongue; he has made it his own and wields it as a tool or weapon. Yet it should be pointed out that this is a "mastery" enacted in the semiotic register rather than the symbolic, a gift for wordplay rather than a capacity for semantic production, with Dass's acts of punning, the irruption of the semiotic into language, prefiguring his own "mutinous" act of braining Jukes, and leaving him for dead. In other words, it is striking that Kipling combines in a single figure an association with the exuberant, irrepressible energies of presymbolic language with an unexpected capacity for treachery against the figure of the sahib.

I emphasize here what I see as Kipling's depiction of discrete (separate and unequal) registers or modalities of language first of all because of the way it suggests the complication (as well as the substantial realization) of older projects of Indian assimilation in the later nineteenth century. A half-century before Kipling wrote his Indian stories, Thomas Macaulay delivered his 1835 "Minute on Indian Education." It is hardly a politically correct document, certainly when viewed from our twenty-first-century vantage point, but two moments in the Minute have earned special opprobrium in our time, each vying for the title of "Macaulay's infamous statement."[22] The first is the well-known line about the "single shelf of a good European library" outweighing the entirety of Oriental literature (Macaulay, *Macaulay*, 722). Works written in Sanskrit and Arabic Macaulay blithely dismisses as a mass of superstitious hokum, mediocre poetry, and sheer bunk, containing "medical doctrines, which would disgrace an English farrier,—Astronomy, which would move laughter in girls at an English boarding school,—History, abounding with kings thirty feet high and reigns thirty thousand years long,—and Geography, made up of seas of treacle and seas of butter" (ibid., 723). But it is the second popular candidate for this particular title that I want to focus on here. This is (and has long been) his assertion that "We must at present do our best to form a class who may be interpreters between us and the millions whom we govern; a class of persons, Indian in blood and colour, but English in taste, in opinions, in morals, and in intellect" (ibid., 729). In Macaulay's vision— shared by men like Charles Trevelyan, his future brother-in-law—this buffer caste was to be created primarily through (English) language education ("Less than half the time which enables an English youth to read Herodotus and Sophocles, ought to enable a Hindoo to read Hume and Milton" [ibid.]).

Offensive, at least to modern sensibilities, the Macaulayan formula may be; I mean to sidestep here the debate over the extent to which it deserves to be called "infamous."[23] But it is interesting to note that *conceptually* Macaulay seems to be able to distinguish between "blood" and "language" in a way that would become far more difficult in the later nineteenth century: he has no trouble imagining that one might be mentally formed by the English tongue while remaining unequivocally "Indian [or anything else, for that matter] in blood" (729). The Anglicists of the day were in other words untroubled, for the most part, by the kind of conceptual conflation or collapse for which Victorian information systems, and the conceptual metaphors that became attached to them involving circulatory and other biological systems, would be largely responsible. But once these metaphors became dominant—at a moment in history, that is, at which it seemed natural to imagine networks as closed systems facilitating the free intermingling of blood (via the conceptual metaphor BLOOD = (TELEGRAPHIC) LANGUAGE)[24]—then the old Anglicist formulations became increasingly problematic. One explanation, then, for Kipling's proto-Kristevan discovery or invention of a hierarchized "division of labour" within language lies in the fact that it offers another way to conceptualize difference between two races, linked within a single language network. If, in other words, the native telegrapher functioned as (among other things) a figure for the Anglicized Indian in the later nineteenth century, then—in Kipling's treatment at least—his depiction also resonates with efforts to ensure that the British-enculturated native remain plainly legible as a figure, in Homi Bhabha's phrase, for "which to be Anglicized, is *emphatically* not to be English" ("Of Mimicry and Man," 125).

Yet there is no denying that the prospect of networking with natives remained troubling to Kipling. If (as I have already suggested) the native operator is often an uncanny figure in his fiction, this fact may not be unrelated to a profound ambivalence towards the idea of such linkage. In his autobiographical *Something of Myself*, while giving a retrospective account of his newspaper days, Kipling recalls a circuit of telecommunications which he would daily enact in concert with an unseen Indian counterpart, both of them constituting relays in a cybernetic system comprising telegraphic, telephonic, Indian and British components: "I took them [cabled messages] down from the telephone—a primitive and mysterious power whose native operator broke every word into monosyllables" (30). The association of the telephone with the "primitive" is both counterintuitive and suggestive; as employed by the "native operator" who seems naturally to belong to its "mysterious" dispensation, it works to break messages, whatever their particular semantic value, about which the speaker seems unconcerned or ignorant, into basic phonemic units. (Another example, perhaps the first, of Kipling's "semiotic" native.) Is it fanciful to suggest that this figure may be the prototype of the Indian charlatan in Kipling's later story "In the House of Suddhoo"? There the native figure, casting his voice by a ventriloquism resembling an uncanny form of telephony into "the dried, shrivelled, black head of a native baby," converts messages secretly gleaned from telegrams into a strikingly similar modality, one that fills the English narrator with horror: "There was an interval of a second or two between each word, and a sort of 'ring, ring, ring,' in each note of the voice, like the timbre of a bell. It pealed slowly, as if talking to itself, for several minutes before I got rid of my cold sweat" (*Plain Tales*, 112–13).[25] This scene forcibly strikes one as a kind of nightmarish restaging of the younger Kipling's habitual telephonic link with the native operator, one in which a certain ambivalence, at the very least, might be detected towards the experience.[26]

The above two figures, then—the uncanny, unseen native on the phone and the eerie ventriloquist—suggest the possibility of a parasitic appropriation from, or insertion into, British information networks. Even they, however—like the other figures I have cited—remain visibly (or audibly) distanced from the language they channel by their innately "semiotic" relation to it: both parse or (as Kipling puts it) "break" English up unnaturally (sentences into isolated words, and words into fragmentary phonemes, respectively). So far, then, the story is a familiar one: the Anglicized Indian does not fully or "really" possess the language, a condition mirroring his partial, subordinate status within the networks of the Indian empire. Here, however, a further question naturally arises: where (if we have here to do with the stuff of classic racialist-imperialist fantasy) is one to find the logically corollary figure, the Englishman in unproblematic possession of the voice of empire, the natural agent of the symbolic order?

What one encounters instead in Kipling (and perhaps, given the thinkers I have invoked in this chapter, this story will not be an entirely unfamiliar one either) is the figuration of imperial power as something that no one, of whatever race, truly or ultimately "possesses." And once more Kipling's treatment of the telegraph—specifically, his depiction of telegraphic language—is enlightening here. At the *Civil and Military Gazette* in Lahore, the young Kipling soon became intimately familiar with the characteristic language ("technolect"?) of the wire, as the lion's share of his duties seemed to involve the reception, sifting, and arrangement of cables, the creation of a kind of telegraphic pastiche ("I write, so to speak, between the horns of the gum pot and the scissors," as he complains to a correspondent in his early days at the paper [quoted in *Kipling's India*, 3]). Unlike Hemingway, though, who seemed to transfer the telegraph's sense of condensation and standardization into his fiction, Kipling's prose explodes, perhaps compensatorily, with a Babel of languages, dialects, idiolects, remarkable and odd names, and so on.[27] But within this polyglot milieu the telegraph can be counted on to speak a radically pared language, a classic form of "cablese"—its elliptical fragments of utterance punctuating, and to be contrasted with, the proliferation of diverse voices that surround it in the text. It seems indeed to represent a kind of asymptotic limit, a condensed language that no person could actually speak. The telegraphic "voice" in Kipling is abstracted from any individual speaker, seeming to possess an inhuman, or at least an impersonal, autonomy, as in "Only a Subaltern":

The message flashed to the Hill stations.—"Cholera—Leave stopped—Officers recalled." Alas for the white gloves in the neatly-soldered boxes, the rides and the dances and picnics that were to be, the loves half spoken, and the debts unpaid! (*Man Who Would Be King*, 16)

The austere "flash[es]" of information, like the authority they represent, seem to be detached from any localizable entity or power—an apt voice for the transpersonal "Other" of Empire (such as that invoked in Steel's novel). Even where a "tar" ("wire") has a determinate sender and recipient, its very abbreviation of expression tends to depersonalize the message, as in "The Bridge-Builders": "Heavy rains here. Bad," runs one message (prompting the musing that it could have been cut still further: "He might have saved the last word" [Kipling, *Day's Work*, 14]). The abridged language of the wire, shorn of identifying idiolect, seems to belong to no one.[28]

Such an impression is only reinforced when one looks more closely at precisely what elements of language are characteristically elided in such maximally terse utterances. Messages like "Cholera—Leave stopped—Officers recalled," and "Heavy rains here. Bad," omit a number of lexical units—articles, for example, and in these cases, verbs. But more significantly, when the telegraph speaks in these stories it is in a language without pronouns, precisely that feature which Emile Benveniste identifies as common to *all* languages:

It is a remarkable fact—but who would notice it, since it is so familiar?—that the "personal pronouns" are never missing from among the signs of a language, no matter what its type, epoch, or region may be. A language without the expression of person cannot be imagined. ("Subjectivity in Language," 730)

But in fact this absence is a defining characteristic of telegraphic language, certainly as Kipling represents it. Benveniste is, of course, concerned with pronouns chiefly in their relation to human subjectivity, their power (in his view) to help construct identity by offering positionality within a structure. As he famously puts it, "Language is so organized that it permits each speaker to appropriate to himself an entire language by designating himself as I" (ibid.). In Kipling's treatment, then, telegraphic language not only suggests the transpersonal voice of empire, speaking through native relays to the Englishmen at its interstices; it implies that those very interstices might have something to do with producing the white men it is calling upon to take up the imperial burden. More, this vast, distributed machine of interpellation, with its enthymematic language shot through with pronomial gaps to be filled by action, tends to destabilize the very categories of "nature" on which British hegemony ostensibly depends.

And indeed, Kipling suggests in one story that the imperial network, figured as telegraphic system, has the power quite literally to make Englishmen, or white men, out of natives, in case of extreme need. This at least seems to be the suggestion of "His Chance at Life," whose central figure, Michele D'Cruze, is a native operator whose position (predictably, as I have tried to show, for this character type) gives him a sense of participation and status as an ersatz Englishman. His employment as a signaler causes his beloved's mother (pathologically invested in her own family's "descent from a mythical [English] platelayer") to be "lenient to the shortcomings of his ancestors" (Kipling, *Plain Tales,* 60). Significantly, however, Michele does himself possess (a negligible modicum of) English blood; we read that while he is "very black," he "looked down on natives as only a man with seven-eighths native blood in his veins can" (ibid.). This formulation prefigures the great event of his life. Having been appointed to a minor relay-station in the sticks, he resigns himself to scrimping and saving (his sweetheart's mother approves of his position as a cog in the imperial machine, but insists that he earn at least 50 rupees a month before he marry her daughter). Nothing much happens at his post until, one day, the locals decide to raise a "Donnybrook just to see how far they could go" (ibid., 62). This is the Mutiny in miniature, or the Mutiny replayed as farce—enacted on a purely local scale, and denuded of all political content. Nonetheless, the rioters select a familiar target for their wrath:

> The Native Police Inspector ran in and told Michele that the town was in an uproar and coming to wreck the Telegraph Office . . . [the Inspector], afraid, but obeying the old race-instinct which recognizes a drop of white blood as far as it can be diluted, said, "What orders does the Sahib give?"
>
> The "Sahib" decided Michele. Though horribly frightened, he felt that, for the hour, he, the man with the Cochin Jew and the menial uncle in his pedigree, was the only representative of English authority in the place. (ibid.)

The Police Inspector's act of interpellation, his recognition of the telegraph operator as "the Sahib" in town, is subsequently echoed and reinforced by that of the telegraphic network, which, in effect, *makes* him a "Sahib." Michele sends a message for help up the line, thereby asserting a position—albeit a highly provisional one—within the colonial system, which in turn recognizes him, as do the townspeople, as the embodiment of "Authority"; he has gone from being a mere relay to a point of origin. His "drop of white blood" is activated, transforming him, for the duration of the riot, into a quasi-Englishman. When confronted by a local delegation, he tells them, haughtily, "that the Sub-Judge might say what he pleased, but, until the Assistant Collector came, the Telegraph Signaller was the Government of India in Tibasu. . . . Then they bowed their heads and said, 'Show mercy!' . . . and went back in great fear; each accusing the other of having begun the rioting" (ibid., 63). Michele's tenure as an Englishman is, again, transitory: when the white "Collector-Sahib" arrives at last to deal with the rioters, the signaler "[feels] himself slipping back more and more into the native" . . . until "the white drop in [his] veins [dies] out" (ibid.). But he is rewarded, in the story's ironized fairy-tale ending, with promotion to the central office, and "the Imperial salary of sixty-six Rupees a month" (ibid.). Michele and his sweetheart are able to marry, "and now there are several little D'Cruzes sprawling about the verandas of the Central Telegraph Office" (ibid.). The story thus ends with a tableau in which symbolic and biological reproduction are mingled, with the prospect of a future line of dutiful imperial servants being embodied in the host of "little D'Cruzes" spawned within the shadow of the central nexus of the British colonial network in India.

Herb Sussman suggests that "[i]f Kipling had remained in India, it is unlikely that he would have been tempted to create a literature of the machine," noting that "[h]is rare newspaper descriptions of technology in India, like Dickens' journalistic pieces on the machine, are written in the manner of the technological grotesque, with little concern for social criticism or symbolic meaning" (Sussman, *Victorians and the Machine*, 195). As regards the world of mechanical invention in the sense of steam engines, locomotives, ships, and so on, this may well be true, but, as I have sought to show here, it was emphatically not the case with Kipling's treatment of information technologies. On the contrary, his Indian fiction to a large extent constitutes a kind of romance of information systems—a body of writing in which media technologies and networks contribute actively to the construction of the author's vision of colonial India.

CHAPTER TWO

e⁄℗

IMPERIAL PROJECTIONS

I.

Having narrowly escaped massacre at the hands of a troop of knife-wielding "Kukuanas"—the mythical, "lost" African race featured in Rider Haggard's *King Solomon's Mines* (1885)—the fast-thinking, polytropic Allan Quatermain improvises a *Große Lüge* of Hitlerian scale and audacity. Flashing "an imperial smile," Quatermain tells the Kukuanas that he and his friends are extraterrestrials, visitors from outer space: "We come from another world, though we are men such as ye; we come . . . from the biggest star that shines at night" (Haggard, *King Solomon's Mines*, 114); thereafter the three Britons (and their African ally) are treated respectfully as "sons of the stars," who voyage, as Quatermain says, "through realms of air" (ibid., 130).

To a people bounded, like other lost races in Haggard's imperial romances, in a veritable geographic nutshell, the reality might have seemed hardly less miraculous: the fact, that is, that the white men have used global networks of transport, including railway and steamer, to travel (in the case of Henry Curtis and Captain Good) from Yorkshire to the heart of Africa. Quatermain's outrageous fib thus expresses a truth, if in wildly hyperbolic form: these representatives of Britain's global empire are indeed space travelers, and prodigious ones. By contrast, in the radically circumscribed kingdom of the Kukuanas, time reigns supreme—a truth brought home to the horrified Englishmen when they discover the dead kings of the Kukuanas, preserved for eternity: "They were human forms . . . or rather had been human forms; now they were stalactites. This was the way in which the Kukuana people had from time immemorial preserved their royal dead" (ibid., 268). As so often in Haggard, the basic mise-en-scène of the narrative might thus be described as a great clash or collision of what Mikhail Bakhtin has termed chronotopes.[1] And as so often in British fiction of the period, this clash, and these chronotopes, are largely figured in terms of technologies—ancient and modern—of communication, transportation, and information capture.

This chapter and the one following share a particular concern with the role played by information technologies in shaping conceptions of colonial and imperial space and time during the heyday of the British Empire. That information systems, most conspicuously the electric telegraph, *did* radically transform forms of spatiotemporal apprehension and experience in manifold ways has of course been a cliché since the days of the Victorians themselves. The phrase "to annihilate space and time" (in some variant) rapidly and enduringly established itself as a highly (and no doubt tiresomely) successful cultural meme in the nineteenth century. This meme is still available for adaptation today, as by Carolyn Marvin in her elucidation of late-Victorian fantasies of cultural homogeneity, in a chapter entitled "Annihilating Space, Time, and Difference" (Marvin, *Old Technologies,* 191–231). And, as historian Duncan Bell has shown, the widespread perception of networks of telegraph, rail, and steam as "dissolving distance" (Bell, *Idea of Greater Britain,* 523) played a crucial role in the emergence, within nineteenth-century political (particularly imperialist) discourse, of a new conception of global space.[2] The basic conceptual metaphor at work here gained, if anything, in robustness during the twentieth century (think McLuhan's "global village") and remains alive and well in the twenty-first.

This particular narrative—which is, again, the product of a collective act of conceptual integration by which an increasingly networked planet was seen as a more easily graspable one mentally[3]—was (and is) thus an influential one, to be sure, and I will not ignore it here. (As I will show, popular novelist Marie Corelli went Sir John Seeley and other propagandists of expansion one better by imaginatively shrinking not merely the globe but the universe itself.) But it was certainly not the only one available to, or explored by, writers of the period. Accordingly, in order fully to trace the multiple ways in which Britons used media to conceive spatial and temporal configurations in the age of Empire, one needs to be cautious about reducing all such accounts to a single master narrative. For the late Victorian novel, even (or especially) in its less intellectually respectable forms (adventure, romance, science fiction) often imagined complex and nuanced, as well as ideologically charged, constellations of imperial time and space which do not, as I hope to show, always fit neatly into such a paradigm.

Any modern attempt to chart the relationship between media technologies and the spatiotemporal matrices associated with particular imperial systems owes a debt, however indirect, to the work of Canadian economic historian Harold Innis.[4] In a pair of highly suggestive, if hardly pellucid, works written at the end of what had to that point been a more or less conventional scholarly career, Innis elaborated a boldly original theory of history premised upon the determining power of media, and particularly upon their tendency to shape imperial systems. These texts—*Empire and Communications* (1950) and *The Bias of Communication* (1951)—argued, among other things, that the destinies of particular empires are rooted in their dependence upon technologies of communication that tilt toward control of (respectively) space or time. Empires whose power is largely predicated upon the mastery of "space-biased" media (the light, portable documents of the Roman imperium, for instance) tend to be expansionist, exerting influence over vast stretches of territory—but doomed to collapse, insufficiently grounded in tradition. Those empires, on the other hand, most characterized by the use of "time-biased" media (the graven stone and spoken word of Egypt, for instance: relatively immobile technologies fostering respect for tradition) may not sprawl, but they will tend to endure. The most stable systems, for Innis, are those that balance spatial and temporal orientations.

There are, to be sure, numerous objections to be made against the conclusions Innis draws regarding particular empires and their systems of communication; more broadly, it is fair to say that his project is probably of limited value *qua* historiography—insofar, that is, as it makes real-world claims about the destinies of imperial systems. Again, I am myself far more interested in the figurative or conceptual status of such technologies within works of fiction. But the basic problematic sketched within Innis's late work suggests a way of thinking, and of writing, about media in relation to spatiotemporal configurations that I have found consistently suggestive. And as my above invocation of the concept of the chronotope indicates, I also rely in both this chapter and the next on the work of Bakhtin. For all their obvious differences, the work of both of these thinkers encourages the critic to develop sophisticated and flexible models for thinking about how writers imagine spatial and temporal forms; and such models are, I think, of crucial importance if one is adequately to delineate the manifold and nuanced ways in which such forms were conceptualized during the age of imperialism.

The remainder of this chapter, then, can be seen as an attempt to delineate—and to juxtapose—two very distinct, though similarly media-inflected, visions of empire. I will primarily discuss two more or less exactly contemporaneous novels—Marie Corelli's *A Romance of Two Worlds* and H. Rider Haggard's *She*—which, read alongside one another, provide a sense of at least some of the multiple varieties of imperial enthusiasm and anxiety alike which it was possible to conceive at one particular historical moment. Where the following chapter, which focuses on the writing of H. G. Wells, takes a close-up view of the final few years of the Victorian age, the present one thus constitutes a kind of snapshot of 1886—a year which, seen as a kind of freeze-frame of history, sits squarely within the salad days of the age of high imperialism. Britons in the latter half of the 1880s could look immediately back at such events as the British acquisition of control of the Suez Canal (and subsequent occupation of Egypt), the revolt of the Mahdi,[5] and a good deal of European "scrambling" in Africa and elsewhere; meanwhile, influential new works of imperial self-reflection were beginning to appear.[6]

Viewed, moreover, in relation to media history, this was a no less dynamic time. Certainly the story of seemingly unlimited telegraphic expansion across the planet, discussed above, deserves prominent mention in any account of technological development covering the years immediately preceding the mid-1880s. As I will show, at the time Corelli conceived her distinctive form of romance novel (and not by accident), the development of submarine telegraphy had led to the association of wired communication with extension across a truly global space (as well as an association with imperial projects in particular). But to focus exclusively on this development would be to ignore the extent to which the media ecology in developed nations like Great Britain was evolving in other ways as well. Technologies attuned to other sensory modalities began to appear: the telephone, for instance, was invented in the 1870s. It is important to remember that, in the latter decades of the century in particular, expansion in space was not the only game in town when it came to media evolution. I am particularly interested here in the emergence in the 70s and 80s of new inscriptive media like the phonograph,[7] as well as the many and diverse experiments in the photographic capture of motion which would culminate in the invention of the cinema—media which Innis would consider to be essentially and massively time-biased. Writers of this period concerned with media thus had to reckon with a complex, and highly fluid, technological ecology.

I hope to show that in these two contemporaneous novels—and Corelli's is, I believe, no less deserving than Haggard's of the title of "imperial romance,"[8] albeit one conceived in a very different key—many of the emergent features of this ecology register in powerful ways. Specifically, where Corelli draws primarily upon spatially oriented technologies in order imaginatively to project the imperial realities of the day onto a literally universal canvas, Haggard's interest in both old and new media of temporal mastery, including the emergent technologies of cinema, leads him to explore not only issues of colonial expansion but also the (equally timely) themes of imperial ephemerality and durability.

II.

Why was Queen Victoria so devoted to the novels of Marie Corelli? For this fact—that Corelli's biggest, or at least most prominent, fan was the nominal ruler (as the hoary formula has it) of a quarter of the world's population and a fifth of its territory—remains one of the few things that, even today, people who know little else about the once phenomenally popular novelist are likely to know about her. Victoria's attachment to Corelli's fiction can be traced to the novelist's first published work, *A Romance of Two Worlds* (1886), a special presentation copy of which the Queen requested from Corelli's publisher, George Bentley (Masters, *Now Barabbas Was a Rotter*, 104). (Bentley would later talk Corelli out of blazoning a sequel, *The Soul of Lilith* [1892], with the words ACCEPTED BY HER MAJESTY THE QUEEN [ibid., 105].) Subsequently, Victoria had the novelist's new productions sent to Balmoral (ibid., 7), and may have even invited her for an overnight stay at Windsor (ibid., 106). The popular association of the Queen with Corelli and her work was widespread: one contemporary journalist reported that "The Queen is supposed to sleep with Miss Corelli's latest story under her pillow" (adding unkindly, "perhaps by way of a soporific"), and a modern biographer suggests that "the reading public realised that Marie was in some way the literary counterpart of their own dear queen" (ibid., 106–7). Moreover, the associative link between the two women would prove durable: one mid-twentieth-century history of the British Empire, for instance, contains the gibe: "the Queen read Marie Corelli. The heir to the throne read nothing" (Adams, *Empire on the Seven Seas*, 228).

The usual explanation for the Queen's passionate attachment to such works as *A Romance of Two Worlds* and *Ardath: The Story of a Dead Self* (1889) lies in their elaboration, and celebration, of a shared moral code, that inflexible system of Christian morality which would come to be called "Victorian." Additional motives of gender solidarity seem plausible as well: as the introduction to a 1970s reprint of *Romance* (appearing under the sign of esoterica, for years perhaps the only publishing niche hospitable to her work) suggests:

That Queen Victoria is said to have preferred Marie Corelli's novels to those of any other writer of her time, despite the carping criticism of "bad style" on the part of the literary pundits of the day, is perhaps largely attributable to the Queen's appreciation of a courageous, forthright, creative woman, successful in a profession dominated largely by men. (Allen, 2)

I want to argue here for a further potential source of attraction on the part of the reigning monarch: one belonging to the domain of the properly political, and thus complicating rather than negating the above motivations. To be sure, explicit references to the political realities of the day are relatively scarce, and sometimes veiled (if very thinly), in texts like *A Romance of Two Worlds* (which I will focus on here). Yet Corelli's ethereal fantasies of the spirit world, though ostensibly far removed from the cut and thrust of party politics in Westminster, or the sordidly practical problems of colonial administration in India or the recently (if unofficially) annexed Egypt, are no less historically grounded in such real-world contexts than are the Palliser novels, or the adventures of Allan Quatermain. Specifically, I want to explore the ways in which the reality of British colonialism registers in *Romance,* in the context of a kind of cyberfantasy of female participation in the vicarious pleasures of imperialist expansion.

In teasing out the novel's (mostly coded) imperial affinities, one might begin by looking at an especially revealing passage to be found midway through the novel. The unnamed narrator of *Romance,* a female musician (an "improvisatrice" [Corelli, *Romance,* 91] whose channeling of celestial harmonies is indebted, as Jill Galvan shows, to contemporary ideas about female mediumship),[9] has sought a cure for her disordered nervous system from a "physical electrician" (ibid., 80), the charismatic Casimir Heliobas. One day, while playing the organ, she is unexpectedly assailed by a pang of religious doubt ("Was Christ indeed Divine—or is it all a myth, a fable— an imposture?") and flees the scene in anxious "terror" (ibid., 132). Heliobas appears, and sternly chastises her for her "[u]nbelief," in a rebuke which also gives him the opportunity to vent his spleen against her country of origin (or at least residence; she is, like Corelli herself, somewhat vague about her background):

And you have come freshly from a land where, in the great Senatehouse, a poor perishable lump of clay calling itself a man, dares to stand up boldly and deny the existence of God, while his compeers, less bold than he, pretend a holy displeasure, yet secretly support him—all blind worms denying the existence of the sun; a land where so-called Religion is split into hundreds of cold and narrow sects, gatherings assembled for the practice of hypocrisy, lip-service and lies—where Self, not the Creator, is the prime object of worship; a land, mighty once among the mightiest, but which now, like an overripe pear, hangs loosely on its tree, awaiting but a touch to make it fall! A land—let me not name it;—where the wealthy, high-fed ministers of the nation slowly argue away the lives of better men than themselves, with vain words of colder and more cruel force than the whirl-ing spears of untaught savages! (ibid., 133)

At one level Heliobas's rant, with its obvious references both to the parliamen-tary saga involving the atheist Charles Bradlaugh and to the "murder of Gor-don"[10] (two events which were, in 1886, very recent history indeed), is simply a passionate screed against the activities of a Liberal Parliament during the previous half-decade. Accordingly, it is not very difficult to imagine the Queen nodding in righteous approval while reading partisan outbursts like the above (though Gladstone himself, if he perceived such jabs, would appear to have forgiven them readily enough, since he became an equally warm admirer of Corelli's fiction).[11]

But it is the ground-note of imperialist ideology underlying the above outburst that may be most crucial to an understanding of the novel's potent, if coded, resonances for readers like Victoria. Besides the angry lament for the martyred Gordon (a theme to which Corelli, again through Heliobas, will return at the end of the novel), the passage also sounds a warning note of imperial decay, of a kind that would become yet more common a decade or so later: England, "mighty once," is now figured as an "overripe pear . . . await-ing but a touch to make it fall" (ibid.). Particularly when bracketed by the other two references to recent parliamentary activity, this would seem an unmistakable condemnation of the Gladstonian antagonism to projects of imperial expansion, previously championed by Disraeli.[12] Furthermore, by juxtaposing contemporaneous scenarios springing from the ostensibly dis-tinct evils of atheism and anti-imperialist insularity, Corelli's sage appears to seek, as if through the white heat of his rage, to fuse them together. If transi-tions are not supplied to smooth the rocky conceptual journey from Brad-laugh to Gordon, by way of the themes of England's denominational diversity and threatened imperial decline, it is surely because they are thought unnec-essary (by Heliobas, by Corelli, and, perhaps, by ideological fellow-travelers like Victoria)—all are, at bottom, symptoms of the same pernicious lack of (Christian or imperialist) faith. In other words, Heliobas's far-roving chain of associative thought only seems incoherent if it is not recognized as a manifestation of one of the text's central acts of blending: namely the collapse of two forms of religious or quasi-religious belief into a single entity.

Recognition of this core conceptual conflation (of atheism with insularity, and—correspondingly—Christian faith with imperialist ardor) is crucial, I would argue, to a full understanding of Corelli's conception of the central trope of her Heliobas novels: a seemingly infinite Christian empire figured as a literally universal telegraphic network. This conceit first appears in *A Romance of Two Worlds,* which invites the reader to accompany its heroine as, under the electrical influence of Heliobas, she is sent on a disembodied voyage through the cosmos, which is revealed as a vast communications system with the Christian God—"a Shape of pure Electric Radiance" (Corelli, *Romance,* 222)—at its center. The premised existence of this network allows Corelli, through Heliobas and his disciples, to elaborate her "Electric Creed," a rewriting of Christian doctrine in terms of the new electric media of the nineteenth century. Reading a document given her by Heliobas titled "The Electric Principle of Christianity," the heroine is vouchsafed a true understanding of the events and principles of which the conventional revelatory account of Christianity constitutes a coded version. God, she learns, is "The All-Fair Beneficent Ruler" of a "great Electric Circle" (ibid., 221, 225), from which humanity has become progressively estranged, by not only an ignorant denial of its spiritual nature but also the sheer distances involved (salvation, it appears, is largely a technological problem):

> [F]rom its position in the Universe, [the earth] receives a less amount of direct influence from the Electric Circle than other worlds more happily situated. Were men wise enough to accept this fact, they would foster to the utmost the germs of electric sympathy within themselves, in order to form a direct communication . . . between this planet and the ever-widening Ring, so that some spiritual benefit might accrue to them thereby. (ibid., 224)

To this end, the benighted human race has been divinely imbued with an innate, if inchoate, yearning to be connected with "a Being greater than [itself]"—a universal instinct that Corelli calls "God's first thought of the cable to be hereafter laid—a lightning-thought which He instilled into the human race to prepare it, as one might test a telegraph-wire from house to house, before stretching it across a continent" (ibid., 225). In keeping with Corelli's overarching conceptual metaphor, the "Electric Theory of Christianity" further recasts Christ as a cosmic relay or go-between: "by His reascension into Heaven He established that much needed electric communication between us and the Central Sphere" (ibid., 227). Even Corelli's advocacy (via Heliobas) of the denomination best suited to facilitate this communion with the Godhead (presumably Catholicism, though this is not explicitly stated) is defended on purely technical, rather than doctrinal, grounds: "I should choose [the church] which has *most electricity* working within it . . . a Church which holds, as it were, the other end of the telegraphic ray between Earth and the Central Sphere" (ibid., 235, emphasis original). Presumably, within such a dispensation, a Clerk Maxwell or a Claude Shannon, equipped to grapple with practical problems of bandwidth, signal strength, and the like, would be fitter candidates for canonization than men like Aquinas or Anselm, who squander their intellectual energies in quibbling over abstruse points of theology.

Of course, the trope of a universal telegraphic network (though it is by no means clear that Corelli considered it a *trope* at all; in her prefaces she is as stout in her defense of the "Electric Creed" as literal fact as are her fictional mouthpieces) is firmly rooted in the historical moment at which Corelli wrote. Transparently a fantasy transposition of the web of gutta-percha-coated cables then being stretched across the planet as fast as steamships could lay them on the ocean floor, Corelli's Christian network is conceptually indebted not (only) to electric communication in general but to submarine telegraphy—the "grand Victorian technology"[13]—in particular. This connection is indeed repeatedly, and explicitly, made within the text:

> "Of course I [Heliobas] am able also to cure those who are *not* by nature connected with me; but then I have to *establish* a connection, and this takes time, and is sometimes very difficult to accomplish, almost as tremendous a task as the laying down of the Atlantic cable." (ibid., 94, emphasis original)

> At one time people mocked at the wild idea that a message could flash in a moment of time from one side of the Atlantic to the other by means of a cable laid under the sea; now that it is an established fact, the world has grown accustomed to it, and has ceased to regard it as a wonder. Granting human electricity to exist, why should not a communication be established, like a sort of spiritual Atlantic cable, between man and the beings of other spheres and other solar systems? (ibid., 164–65)

> "In brief, this Earth and God's World were like America and Europe before the Atlantic Cable was laid. Now the messages of goodwill flash under the

waves, heedless of the storms. So also God's Cable is laid between us and His Heaven in the person of Christ." (ibid., 225)

And when Heliobas muses that "Shakespeare's *girdle round the earth*' foretold the electric telegraph" (ibid., 135, emphasis original), he can of course only have the global system of submarine cables in mind. (That this manmade "girdle" may constitute a rudimentary, or prosthetic, component of the divine network is suggested by its similarity to the "electric belt," visible even from earth, which circles Saturn, bestowing health on the more spiritually advanced inhabitants of the planet [ibid., 177].)

Given that Corelli imagines connections across vast distances between equals, or at least fellow Christians (albeit of varying degrees of spiritual evolution), the repeated references to the Atlantic cable (laid first in 1858, and enduringly in 1866) are probably inevitable, perhaps conceptually necessary. But two decades had passed since the successful forging of the Anglophone link between Britain and America, decades which had witnessed not only the emergence of a truly global cable network—a system that would in time penetrate, as it must have seemed, virtually every corner of the inhabited world—but also a fundamental transition in the way that network was conceptualized. Specifically, the telegraphic web which more and more truly came to approximate the world-circling "girdle" envisioned by Corelli had acquired an inescapably imperial character. By the time Corelli wrote her first novel, European—especially British—wires stretched to countless shores besides those inhabited by North American interlocutors: Britain and India were reliably connected in 1870, and within the next fifteen years electric tentacles were tugging Southeast Asia, the Far East, Australia and New Zealand, South America, and Africa (including Southern Africa) ever closer to the centers of imperial power and influence (Headrick, *Tools of Empire,* 161). Moreover, during the previous half-decade in particular the interests of empire had come decidedly, and conspicuously, to supplant those of commerce within the new network:

> The cable network of the seventies was composed of economic cables, that is to say, lines that were useful to business and private customers. After 1880 such opportunities were depleted, and a new era opened. The Admiralty and the Colonial, War, and Foreign offices had gotten accustomed to communicating by telegram and wished to extend that possibility to all parts of the British Empire. As jingoist sentiments rose, it became increasingly galling to have British telegrams cross non-British territories. Thus, ever

more distant lines with ever less economic value were laid for political reasons. (ibid., 162)

The worldwide web of submarine cables became, indeed, "an essential part of the new imperialism," even, in some cases, actively "help[ing] the empire to expand" (ibid., 163)—and this crucial symbiosis could not fail to leave powerful traces in contemporary accounts of the expanding global "girdle" of electric communication. Certainly, no depiction of a universal (Christian) telegraphic network can, in the later 1880s, have been wholly innocent of imperialist associations.

Nor, indeed, does Corelli shy away from such associations. On the contrary: as I have already indicated, her fiction not only celebrates Christian faith but also tirelessly collapses it with imperialist sentiment, using the figure of electric communication (appropriately enough) to facilitate the necessary conceptual linkage. In the "Prologue" to the original edition of *Romance* she writes openly of "the great empire of the Christian Religion" (Corelli, *Romance*, 16), a system subsequently figured in the novel as "a majestic universal Protectorate" (ibid., 41), a significant term in the history of modern British imperialism. The universe itself thus emerges as a quasi-colonial system in which a supreme "Central Intelligence" (ibid., 221) exercises a benevolent dominion over the multitude of diverse "Kingdoms of the Air" to which it is telegraphically linked ("Thrones, principalities and powers are among them, yet all are equal") (ibid., 49).

Restoring the novel's imperialist affinities renders intelligible, I would argue, much that seems (especially, perhaps, to the modern reader) merely random or incoherent. I would, again, cite in particular Heliobas's two seemingly unmotivated references to Gordon and his 1885 demise (two of the text's very few overt gestures towards the reality of British imperial expansion). The first mention of the imperialist hero is, again, oblique but unmistakable, with Heliobas railing against "the wealthy, high-fed ministers [who] slowly argue away the lives of better men than themselves, with vain words of colder and more cruel force than the whirling spears of untaught savages" (ibid., 133). Then, at the novel's conclusion, after the narrator-heroine has been revivified by her electrical treatments, Heliobas departs mysteriously for Egypt (not only the home of ancient Eastern wisdom but also the newly established nexus of Britain's imperial network). In a parting message to her, he prophesies an event of no more apparent relevance than when it was first invoked, namely, the martyrdom—now represented as imminent rather than past[14]— of Gordon in the Sudan, an event to which he now refers more explicitly:

The capability of Heliobas to foretell future events proved itself in his knowledge of the fate of the famous English hero, Gordon, long before that brave soldier met his doom. At the time the English Government sent him out on his last fatal mission, a letter from Heliobas to me contained the following passage:

"I see Gordon has chosen his destiny and the manner of his death. Two ways of dying have been offered him—one that is slow, painful, and inglorious; the other sudden, and therefore sweeter to a man of his temperament. He himself is perfectly aware of the approaching end of his career; he will receive his release at Khartoum. England will lament over him for a little while and then he will be declared an inspired madman who rushed recklessly on his own doom; while those who allowed him to be slain will be voted the wisest, the most just, and virtuous in the realm." (ibid., 305)

Another swipe at the Gladstonians, and at (little) "England." And once again, Gordon should be seen as a textual anchoring-point in the reality of imperial expansion, as well as a kind of key for decoding its conceptual conflation of Christianity and imperialism: precisely the fusion he himself represented, paradigmatically, within the British imagination. (Interestingly, though the novelist could hardly have known it, Gordon seems independently to have evolved a strikingly Corellian conception of a Christian communications network linking heaven and earth, centered in the Middle East, with Christ as its relay or intermediary.)[15]

Moreover, this prophesy, with its suggestion of a special connection between Heliobas and Gordon across space and time, and of privileged information shared in turn with the narrator (and through her the reader), invokes the figure of a secret, alternate network (with imperialist sympathies) fundamentally antipathetic to the (merely) *English* Government" (ibid., 305, emphasis added). Such a fantasy, along with the pleasures of vicarious participation it offers, deeply informs the novel throughout, and is surely responsible for part of its appeal: from the heroine's first initiation into Heliobas's network she is made privy to knowledge about a host of secrets both on and off this planet, through private channels which include telepathic exchange, the circulation of manuscripts not meant for the public eye, and even the use of a form of secret writing based on "vegetable electricity" (ibid., 300). And Heliobas's electro-spiritual network (which apparently counts men like Gordon among its members[16]), is clearly affiliated with, if not equivalent to, the great Christian "empire" invoked in the novel's preface, where Corelli had deplored the fact that she wrote "[a]t a time when the great empire of the

Christian Religion is being assailed or politely ignored by governments and public speakers" (ibid., 16).

The opposition here between "empire" and "government" is, I think, highly significant. Ostensibly the "two worlds" of Corelli's title refer to the realms of the material and the spiritual, respectively. At another level, however, they can be taken to represent two opposed political entities (themselves aligned by Corelli precisely with the material and the spiritual, respectively). The first is England, conceived as traditional, and decidedly *un*romantic, nation-state, governed by an all-male Parliament which Corelli pointedly associates with materialism, atheism, and provincial insularity (read: anti-imperialism). The second is the emergent conceptual entity whose contours were being delineated during this period of unprecedented imperial expansion, an entity broadly equivalent to the Greater Britain celebrated (again) by writers like Seeley and Dilke. In Corelli's fiction, then, this entity is figured as a boundless, networked space through which Corelli's (largely female) readership was invited to voyage in spirit. She thus offers, in effect, a fantasy of participation within a coded version of the new imperial network, one starkly opposed to the traditional, all-male network associated with parliamentary politics.

Seen in this light, novels like *Romance* seem less to have merely attracted Victoria's favor than positively to have courted it, by structurally rehearsing elements of what might be termed her own (very public) imperial romances—a phrase by which I mean to invoke her relationships both with the empire itself and with one of its most prominent advocates during the previous few decades. For it seems to me that, whether consciously or not, in conceptualizing the figure of Heliobas, Corelli imaginatively transferred to her Near Eastern wizard many of the qualities which the public had come to associate with another Oriental "magician," one who had himself departed from the stage of history in recent memory, namely Disraeli himself. Such a coding or conflation would have a certain appropriateness within the novel's ideological economy: just as, according to my reading, Gladstone is (anonymously) demonized in the text, so is Disraeli (pseudonymously) idealized therein, his better parts crowned, as it were, in Heliobas.[17]

Certainly there are multiple and striking correspondences between Corelli's romanticized Eastern mage and Victoria's recently deceased companion (Disraeli had died five years earlier, in 1881) in what has been termed a "romantic partnership"[18] closely associated with issues of imperial expansion. Like Heliobas, Disraeli was frequently portrayed as a magician figure from the East: Carlyle called him, disparagingly, a "Hebrew conjurer,"[19] Arnold a "charlatan."[20] To Sir John Skelton he was "the potent wizard" (quoted in Hibbert, *Disraeli,* 263). And as Anthony Wohl finds in his study of the representation of Disraeli's Jewishness in political cartoons, the specific trope of magician (other stereotypical figures with which he was associated included Shylock and Satan) became especially prevalent towards the end of his career.[21] Corelli, I want to suggest, may have tapped into these widespread associations in inventing Heliobas, while substituting positive valences for the overwhelmingly negative ones with which these were, in their original context, chiefly freighted. Heliobas's "Chaldean" ancestry, moreover, functions very much as had Disraeli's Jewishness within the popular imagination (not a little thanks to his own efforts): Heliobas boasts of being "pure Chaldee" (Corelli, *Romance,* 74),[22] an "Oriental" (ibid., 221)[23] with a privileged hereditary access to the original wellsprings of Christianity (a version of the argument elaborated in Disraeli's *Tancred*). Furthermore, his "romantic" relationship with the heroine (if it is appropriate so to term it) takes a curiously oblique, but structurally specific, form rather precisely homologous to the relationship between the queen and her favorite minister. Though there does seem to be some degree of erotic "electricity" present, Heliobas is not the narrator's lover but her conduit, a guardian figure who facilitates her entry into vast information networks, enabling her disembodied voyage through seemingly infinite space. There is, surely, a certain resonance here with Disraeli's well-publicized role in offering a vicarious experience of global empire to his homebound monarch, as for instance in his personal "gifts" of a passage to India, in the form of the Suez Canal ("You have it, Madam," as he famously exulted to her) and indeed of India itself, in the form of an Empress's crown.[24] Moreover, if one accepts the identification of Heliobas with Disraeli (or, perhaps, his spirit), the passage about Gordon quoted above invites the construction of a counterfactual scenario that would have spoken strongly to Victoria: if Disraeli had been Prime Minister in the eighties, instead of the reviled "M.O.G.," the "martyr of empire"[25] would also have lived.

Small wonder, then, if Victoria *did* sleep with Corelli under her pillow. Indeed *Romance,* with its unnamed cipher-heroine, can be seen as a veritable technology of royal interpellation, with Victoria's fervent fandom best understood, perhaps, as part of a feedback loop.[26] In any event, Corelli's fiction unquestionably taps into contemporary currents of excitement, inseparable from both the reality and the representation of a radically expanding imperial system, in crafting a powerful fantasy of female participation in global (indeed universal) networks, of a kind impossible within a (still institutionally patriarchal) nation-state. *Romance* should be seen, at least in part, as an experiment in genre, a kind of female imperial romance—an alternately gendered counterpart to the popular, emergent genre associated with authors like Haggard (to whose work I shall now turn), and with a male readership. This experiment, as I have tried to show, derives directly from—would indeed be literally unthinkable without—the parallel, symbiotic development of the British Empire and its media at precisely this historical moment. In a new age of imperialist expansion figured, as it was abetted, by means of electric communication, Corelli's fiction thus suggested that women too might share in the vicarious pleasures of such growth.

III.

In the course of their African adventures, the British protagonists of Rider Haggard's *She* encounter horrors ranging from a tradition of human sacrifice involving a white-hot pot placed over the victim's head to the grotesque demise of the novel's eponymous queen. Yet one revelation that seems to disconcert Holly, the narrator, at least as much as do these is the discovery of an extensive system of ancient canals constructed, as he later learns, by the long-vanished empire of Kôr. The trope of a canalized Africa within a British novel of this time (*She* was written early in 1886, and serialized in '86–'87) was not, of course, without contemporary resonance. The modern Suez Canal, opened in 1869, had in the past decade acquired a new significance in the British imagination, from its dramatic presentation as a personal gift from Disraeli to Victoria in 1875 to its perceived status as the nexus of Britain's imperial communications system, leading to its occupation by British forces in the 1882 Anglo-Egyptian war. But as the classically obsessed Haggard was surely aware, the new center of Britain's global empire had well-documented forerunners in antiquity: the Persian, Egyptian, and other "Suez canals" described by such writers as Pliny, Strabo, Ptolemy, Herodotus, and Aristotle.[27] By indirectly invoking such Eastern antecedents, Haggard delivers a subtle rebuke to unreflective expansionist sentiment, saying, in effect, Africa was networked long before the Europeans got there.

And yet more troubling, of course, is the prospect of a new power emerging from the rubbish-heap or graveyard of those dead networks. Among the other anxieties it exploits, *She* plays upon Western fears of a revivified expansionist power from the East. What I want particularly to explore here is the centrality of media to Haggard's vision of this threatened resurgence, and of the potential clash of oriental and occidental imperial systems. Certainly Kôr, as its extensive system of canals suggests, was once—like the British imperium represented in little by Haggard's adventurers—an empire much concerned with expansion and circulation in space. When Ayesha takes Holly into the subterranean tombs of this vanished civilization, they find inscriptions attesting to the greatness of Kôr's imperial past, before its destruction by plague:

> Kôr is fallen! No more shall the mighty feast in her halls, no more shall she rule the world, and her navies go out to commerce with the world. Kôr is fallen! and her mighty works, and all the cities of Kôr, and all the harbours that she built and the canals that she made . . . Kôr the Imperial is no more. (Haggard, *She*, 179–80)

With its "canals," "harbours," and far-voyaging "navies," Kôr in its heyday thus represented a decidedly space-oriented imperium, its projects of conquest and commerce facilitated by prodigious networks of communication extending far over land and sea. Now, however, its transmissions stretch across time rather than space, its imperial chronotope having suffered a kind of implosion: an empire of space has become an empire of time, its channels of expansion replaced by immobile media of duration.

In tracing such a trajectory Haggard seems, again, to sound a warning note regarding the imperial past, and potentialities, of an essentialized East of which imperial Kôr represents a compression. Kôr is not exactly Persia, Egypt, Babylon, or even China—all civilizations invoked within the text in connection with it—but a blend of the Eastern imperial systems of history. (Its name, networks of maritime commerce, and tragic, immolated queen surely also suggest a connection with Carthage, the counter-empire of Rome.) Only at its peril, the text seems to suggest, does the West regard its colonial possessions (actual or potential) as blank cartographic space. Rather, at least if Haggard's persistent association of the empires of both Kôr and Ayesha with powerfully time-biased media of both the past and (Haggard's) present is any indication, they are more fitly imagined as a congeries of inscriptive media.

Certainly the domains of She are thoroughly saturated with information by means of inscriptions of the traditional sort: the walls of the caves in which Ayesha and her alien subjects live, as well as the gothicized tombs of Kôr, are both carved and painted with iconic signs as well as "extraordinary characters," "more like Chinese writing than any other that I am acquainted with" (Haggard, *She*, 178). Ayesha, who can read a "little . . . of their inscriptions" (ibid.), translates some of the "Chinese-looking hieroglyphics" (ibid., 265) for Holly, telling of the history of this warlike, expansionist race ("They conquered till none were left to conquer") (ibid., 181), and their ultimate doom in the wake of an apocalyptic pestilence. The stone-cut letters, though formed millennia before Egypt, are yet, Holly notes, "so deeply graven as to be still quite legible" (ibid., 265); elsewhere he remarks that the wall-hewn "pictures and writings . . . [are] in many cases absolutely fresh and perfect as the day on which the sculptor had ceased work on them" (ibid., 132–33). As with other time-capsule-like spaces one finds throughout Haggard's imperial adventures (one thinks, for instance, of the cave in *King Solomon's Mines* where the Portuguese treasure-hunter Silvestre's body is preserved intact for centuries [99]), the caves of Kôr are powerfully resistant to the decay of information, preserving not only the "official" inscriptions cut in the enduring medium of stone but also, and even, the graffitic writing of this long-dead civilization: "On the wall was something painted with a red pigment in similar characters to those hewn beneath the sculpture of Tisno, King of Kôr. This long inscription Ayesha translated to me, the pigment still being quite fresh enough to show the form of the letters" (Haggard, *She,* 179). Unlike the perennially (re)translated text on the Greek potsherd passed down by generations of Vinceys (an artifact I shall discuss in more detail below), the inscriptions of Kôr, like its preserved dead, simply endure, defying the millennia.

Moreover, there are numerous echoes in the novel of *modern* technologies associated with temporal mastery, as Haggard draws upon the new inscriptive media of the later (earlier, of course, in the case of photography) nineteenth century in crafting his vision of a potential colonial space charged with memories of an imperial past, shot through with technologies of storage and preservation. Surely, for instance, the special techniques used to preserve the dead of Kôr suggest an art of fixity associated with (still) photography. Saturated with a potent chemical "preservative" (ibid., 184), the bodies of the dead are themselves in effect transformed into three-dimensional simulacra of their living selves.[28] And Haggard's association of time-oriented media with the counter-empires of the East continues in his depiction of the regime of Ayesha, heir and successor to Imperial Kôr. She is herself not without photographic associations—indeed, the very depiction of her eternal preservation is suggestive: she has been fixed in time by the "blinding" flash of a mystic flame (ibid., 289). There are echoes, too, of that paradigmatic inscriptive technology of the "Edison Age," the phonograph, in Ayesha's ability to reproduce spoken Arabic, Latin, and Greek in forms thought inaccessible to the modern ear—the first in a pristine dialect unchanged by language drift, the latter two in "the accent of her contemporaries" (ibid., 175), a form unknown to modern-day scholars.[29]

Above all, *She* is pervaded by what I want to suggest is an essentially cinematic logic.[30] Certainly the historical moment of the novel's conception and appearance was an extraordinarily fertile one in terms of that convergence of visual and kinetic technologies and practices that we, with the benefit of hindsight, term pre- or protocinematic. In Thomas Edison's well-known account of how he came to conceive of what would become the Kinetoscope, he wrote:

> In the year 1887, the idea occurred to me that it was possible to devise an instrument which should do for the eye what the phonograph does for the ear, and that by a combination of the two all motion and sound could be recorded and reproduced simultaneously . . . the germ of [this idea] came from the little toy called the Zoetrope, and the work of Muybridge, Marié [sic], and others. . . . (Dickson, *History*, 3)

The independent chronophotographic projects of Eadweard Muybridge (legendary parser of the horse's gallop) and Étienne-Jules Marey (inventor of a rapid-fire, protocinematic *fusil*) were indeed crucial developments.[31] But these two were not the only figures laboring, at this historical moment, in the fields of chronophotography[32]— nor was Edison the only one to have experienced a cinematic "Eureka!" moment in the late eighties: Louis Aimé Augustin Le Prince "spent the years from 1886 to 1888 developing a [moving-picture] camera and projector" (Ceram, *Archaeology of the Cinema*, 142), while Emile Reynaud patented his projection device, the Théâtre Optique, in 1888 (Mannoni, *Great Art of Light and Shadow*, 377). And if the extent to which his imperial romance of 1886–87 imagines similar technologies is any indication, Haggard's was another of the many creative minds alive, at that time, to the possibility of an art of kinetic capture—an art that parallels or models the novel's central conceit of the indefinite preservation of human life.[33]

The most obvious adumbrations of the cinema in the novel are, no doubt, to be found in those scenes in which Ayesha, mistress of an ancient Eastern science known of old "[i]n Arabia and in Egypt" (Haggard, *She*, 152), demonstrates her ability to project moving "photograph[s]" (ibid., 216), drawn from the memories stored in her own and other minds, onto a surface of water. It is true that Ayesha is capable of projecting scenes that she has not personally witnessed, so long as they have taken place in settings known to her. Nonetheless, her kinetic photography is clearly associated with a logic of storage, the reproduction or recall of past events:

> "The water [as she tells Holly] is my glass. . . . Therein I can show thee what thou wilt of the past, if it be anything that has to do with this country and with what I have known, or anything that thou, the gazer, hast known.

Think of a face if thou wilt, and it shall be reflected from thy mind upon the water. . . . I can read nothing of the future." (ibid., 152)

Later, in an episode in which "dead scene[s]" stored in the Englishmen's minds are brought to life for Ayesha's edification or amusement, Holly reiterates "that She's power in this matter was strictly limited; she could apparently, except in very rare instances, only photograph upon the water what was actually in the mind of someone present" (ibid., 216).

Again: while Haggard is writing at a time just before the birth of the cinema proper, by the later 1880s the idea of moving pictures, and of motion photography in particular, was very much in the air. And the most salient figure in this technological narrative may be (the already-mentioned) Muybridge, whose experiments in the photographic capture of human and animal locomotion—subsequently presented, to great acclaim, to audiences on both sides of the Atlantic—signaled a new technological mastery over time and movement.[34] In 1878 Muybridge had "beg[u]n giving public lectures, illustrated by his images in lantern-slide form—large-scale transparencies, projected onto a screen"; but soon afterwards he would conceive a new device that would "not only . . . show his moments of frozen time one by one but also string them together to re-create living motion on the screen" (Clegg, *Man Who Stopped Time*, 141). This invention was the Zoöpraxiscope, just one of an ever-growing number of devices devoted to the preservation of motion, even, as many of their names (Zootrope or Zoetrope, Bioscope, Biograph, Biokam, Photozoötrope, Vitascope, Viviscope) signaled, of life itself.[35] Ayesha's kinetophotographic device, surely, fits neatly beside such products of late nineteenth-century innovation. But granted an ancient pedigree—as Haggard attributes it to the lost science of an Eastern Other—it becomes another of the inscriptive media the text uses in figuring an imperium of duration.

Moreover, Ayesha's less advanced subjects—the barbarous present-day occupants of Kôr—themselves inhabit a kind of primitive cinematic world, a network of caves whose walls are alive with moving shadows cast by the flickering light of fires and "rude" lamps of native manufacture. Throughout the novel Holly calls the reader's attention to the spectacular nature of these projections, at which he finds himself frequently gazing (he writes of "contemplating [his captors] and [their] huge moving shadows on the rocky walls" (Haggard, *She*, 86); of "staring . . . at the shadows thrown by the flickering earthenware lamps" (ibid., 98); and so on. (Given Haggard's—and his protagonists'—classical predilections, it is tempting to read into such scenes echoes of Plato's similarly shadow-strewn cave as well, since cast as a kind of ur-cinema, poetic forerunner of modern technologies of projection.[36]) That

Haggard thinks of such primitive technologies of projection as essentially time-oriented media, linked with a dispensation of storage and fixity, is suggested by their association with the scenes from the distant past with which, as it emerges, the caves of Kôr are also charged: the episodes of the lives of its former inhabitants which are replayed in the mind with film-like vividness, in the form of hallucinatory visions and dreams.

Given the abundance of such avatars of the cinema throughout the text, it is fitting that Haggard's ur-technology (for such, surely, it is meant to be) associated with the indefinite preservation of life resembles nothing so much as a huge, primal zoetrope—the popular optical device and ancestor of the modern cinema. Having brought Leo, Holly, and Job deep underground, Ayesha bids them "prepare to enter the very womb of the Earth, wherein she doth conceive the Life that ye see brought forth in man and beast—ay, and in every tree and flower" (Haggard, *She*, 286–87). She leads them into a strange cavern, "filled with a soft glow of rose-coloured light," to await the return of the "Heart of Life" which visits the cavern with machine-like regularity (ibid., 287). Indeed, the life-giving "pillar"—described as a rotating cylinder—gives every appearance of being a machine in fact, a kind of huge, gyrating projector, giving off "light beam[s], reaching us in great flashes like the rays from a lighthouse" (ibid.). Each time it appears, Holly stresses its wheel-like nature, first describing it as "an awful cloud or pillar of fire, like a rainbow many-coloured, and like the lightning bright . . . turning slowly round and round" (ibid.). And again:

> "Nearer it came, and nearer yet, till it was close upon us, rolling down like all the thunder-wheels of heaven behind the horses of the lightning. On it came, and with it came the glorious blinding cloud of many-coloured light, and stood before us for a space, turning, as it seemed to us, slowly round and round, and then accompanied by its attendant pomp of sound, passed away I know not whither." (ibid., 288–89)

> "Nearer and nearer it came; now flashes of light, forerunners of the revolving pillar of flame, were passing like arrows through the rosy air; and now the edge of the pillar itself appeared." (ibid., 292)

> "[W]e waited till, turning slow round upon its own axis, it had flamed and thundered by." (ibid., 298)

In its resistless regularity the phenomenon seems to owe something to the poetics of the railway as well ("the thunder-wheels of the Spirit of Life," remarks Holly, "yet rolled upon their accustomed track") (ibid., 295); but again, the resonances with optical technologies would seem especially relevant here.[37] An embodied blend of the vital principle with a technology of turning or troping, Haggard's great wheel of life bears, as I have already suggested, a more than etymological resemblance to the zoetrope ("Greek ζωή life + -τροπος turning") (*OED*),[38] and its cousins, technologies which promised a kind of uncanny extension or preservation of life. And like Ayesha's own gift of eternal life, the cinematic promise of immortality is a deeply ambivalent one, a preservation that is also arrest, and which lies (as she soon learns) perilously near to unlife.

Ayesha's second encounter with the primal wheel of life leads directly, of course, to what is both the novel's climax and, no doubt, its most "cinematic" scene: the hideously accelerated senescence which Haggard figures, famously, as evolutionary retrogression. (Or, as the horrified manservant Job, "in a shrill falsetto of terror," more colorfully expresses it, "she's turning into a monkey!" [ibid., 293].) Certainly the specter of evolutionary reversal could (and can) be a potent enough source of horror in its own right.[39] Given this text's obsession with media of storage, capable of inscribing and preserving forms across vast temporal spans, however, Ayesha's demise takes on an added significance. In a scene that, to our eyes, resembles nothing so much as a film running backwards, Haggard reveals the human form as the ultimate medium of inscription, stored with the records of countless ancestral forms. It is a case of Muybridge meeting Darwin, with grotesque consequences (or, to think of it another way, it is as if the impresario famous for his photographic capture of the life-principle of men and animals respectively[40] has somehow gotten his slides mixed).

But what is one to make of all these media of storage in this imagined corner of Africa? Fundamentally, I think, Haggard wants to suggest that the imperial energies of the East are not dead but sleeping; some such lesson, in any event, would seem to underlie the persistent tropes of convertibility and reversibility that run through the text, of long-stored potential energy actualized in the present, as with the ancient mummies of Kôr used as ghastly torches to illuminate Ayesha's Neronian entertainments. When it is discovered by Holly's little company, Ayesha's empire embodies the precise inversion of Britain's imperial system as it was coming to be conceptualized during this period. Where the British Empire exemplified a process of seemingly unlimited territorial expansion haunted by the specter of extinction, the empire of She marries radically delimited spatial bounds with virtually infinite duration. Ayesha governs a kind of imploded empire, a bounded space filled with petty, internecine squabbles that she is obliged to referee:

I asked what size the land was, and how many people lived in it. She [Ustane] answered that there were ten "Households," like this that she knew of, including the big "Household," where the Queen [Ayesha] was, that all the "Households" lived in caves, in places resembling this stretch of raised country, dotted about in a vast extent of swamp, which was only to be threaded by secret paths. Often the "Households" made war on each other until *She* sent word that it was to stop, and then they instantly ceased. That and the fever which they caught in crossing the swamps prevented their numbers from increasing too much. They had no connection with any other race, indeed none lived near them, or were able to thread the vast swamps. Once an army from the direction of the great river (presumably the Zambesi) had attempted to attack them, but they got lost in the marshes . . . and half of them were drowned. . . . The marshes, she told us, were absolutely impassable except to those who knew the paths. . . . (Haggard, *She*, 90–91)

And while within her sharply circumscribed empire Ayesha's power, like her knowledge, is virtually absolute (again, her private cinema screen can show her what is happening elsewhere in her realm), there is, until the arrival of Haggard's Britons, little danger of any circulation of bodies or energies between her domain and the world beyond. Everything about the land she rules suggests a logic of temporal preservation, at the expense of territorial expansion. As I have shown already, Haggard depicts the extinct realm of Kôr as a space shot through with time-oriented media of inscription and storage. And as the above quotation indicates, the very land of Kôr is shown to be radically hostile to movement, resistant alike to invasion and exodus. In contradistinction to the dromological, circulatory territory, gridded with roads and canals, engineered by its former imperial masters, Ayesha's empire is now for the most part a treacherous "morass," impossible to traverse at any speed (indeed, nearly impossible to traverse at all)—Holly describes "Miles on miles of quagmire, varied only by bright green strips of comparatively solid ground"; to make matters worse, "the nature of the soil frequently changed . . . so that places which might be safe enough to cross one month would certainly swallow the wayfarer the next" (ibid., 116).[41] Left alone, it is suggested, the ancient energies of the place would likely remain safely stored away, within fixed bounds. But the incursion by the West (in miniature) dramatized by Haggard soon awakens dormant ambitions of territorial conquest. As has been pointed out, *She* represents an early version of the reverse-colonization fantasy, with Ayesha planning parasitically to replace imperial Victoria at the center of Britain's global system: one potential danger, the text seems to suggest, in the increasingly networked, global-ized spaces engendered by the West's own colonial enterprises.[42]

Certainly Western media, the more Ayesha learns of their powers and reach, would have offered a tantalizing prospect to the "imperial" She; it is perhaps less clear whether she might have discerned their affinities (in Hag-gard's treatment) with a form of immortality, and of modes of reproduction, quite alien to the kind which she has herself enjoyed over the centuries. For in contradistinction to his depiction of immobile media of storage, Haggard, from the very beginning of the novel, pointedly aligns the Western imperial tradition with a collection of migratory media, capable of movement across both space and time. When, on his twenty-fifth birthday, Leo Vincey opens the mysterious box that has been transmitted from father to son for millen-nia, he finds an ancient potsherd, "covered . . . with [Greek] writing" (ibid., 26), along with translations of the same text. In all, the narrative originally inscribed on the potsherd is reproduced in its entirety five times in the same chapter: in English, two forms of Greek, and two forms of Latin. There would seem to be little obvious reason for this master of fast-paced narrative not only to imagine, but to reproduce so scrupulously for his readers, such an extreme degree of redundancy. In part it may be surmised that Haggard, who took great pleasure in forging an actual potsherd as well as produc-ing the various translations, was simply enjoying himself. But at the same time the effect of so many incarnations of the "same" text, laid out at tedious length, is to foreground, indeed in some way to enact for the reader, the fun-gible, migratory nature of the information it contains, capable of contingent embodiment in various languages and upon various media, and of prodi-gious migration. It is accompanied by marginal annotations, added by the male members of the family line as they, and the shard, follow the course of Empire in its westward drift. These travel from Greece during the period of its imperial greatness, to imperial Rome, to the domains of Charlemagne, to the imperial England of Elizabeth (and now, Victoria). The shard, a kind of compressed embodiment of the Western imperial impulse, is constantly on the move, not only traversing actual territory but also moving metaphori-cally, through linguistic drift, corruption, translation, and transcription. (Moreover, these mobile media send generation after generation of Vincey men voyaging to Africa, thus setting the narrative itself into motion.) This logic of transmission through re-embodiment mirrors, of course, the novel's conception of reincarnation, the way in which the Kallikrates-Vincey line, in contrast with Ayesha, reproduces itself across the centuries with minimal (outward, at least) variation or hereditary "drift."

In short, *She* is a novel (to put it mildly) much concerned with exploring multiple forms of transmission across both time and space. It has been pointed out that, in *She* and elsewhere, Haggard enjoyed indulging in "fantasies of reproduction without women" (Kucich, "Psychoanalytic Historicism," 102).[43] It is, however, far less certain—at least to judge from the genealogical fantasy cited above—whether he was able to conceptualize reproduction without the accompaniment or agency of media. Just as, for the Vinceys, biological and cultural transmission unfolds in partnership with a migratory, palimpsested potsherd, so, as I have tried to show, does Haggard's conception of imperial systems—their spread and survival—depend substantially on emergent ideas about the potentialities inherent in various media for facilitating, respectively, extension and storage. I want to turn now to a figure who, while far more critical than either Haggard or Corelli of Britain's imperial project, was no less indebted to media for conceptual frames with which to imagine it.

CHAPTER THREE

IMPERIAL TRANSMISSIONS

I.

Reflecting, in his *Outline of History* (1920), upon the past glories of imperial China, and particularly upon its precocious invention of gunpowder, H. G. Wells marvels that the Chinese "[do] not to this day dominate the world culturally and politically" (555). In speculating about the possible causes of this once-great civilization's putative stagnation, Wells rejects any facilely racialist explanation, invoking only to dismiss, for example, the theory of an innately "conservative" Asian brain, biologically predisposed towards cultural stasis. Rather, he locates the seeds of China's "backwardness," and therefore the distal cause of its imperial retrogression, at the level of distributed consciousness—namely, in Chinese *media*, specifically the writing systems which, in Wells's judgment, must inhibit rather than facilitate the kind of advanced thought and action indispensable to a people with designs of global "domination." The symbolic technologies of the Chinese, in other words—their "pictographs, ideograms, and phonograms"—in effect become the tea leaves through whose scrutiny Wells believes he may read the fate of the society that has devised them. Earlier, he had called the Chinese script-system "an instrument which is probably too elaborate in structure, too laborious in use, and too inflexible in its form to meet the modern need for simple, swift, exact, and lucid communications," a fact with ominous implications for its future as a world "power":

Now, it is manifest that here in the Chinese writing is a very peculiar and complex system of sign-writing. A very great number of characters have to be learnt and the mind habituated to their use. The power it possesses to carry ideas and discussion is still ungauged by western standards, but we may doubt whether it will ever be possible to establish such a wide, common mentality as the simpler and swifter alphabets of the western civilizations permit. In China it created a special reading-class, the mandarins, who were also the ruling and official class. Their necessary concentration upon words and classical forms, rather than upon ideas and realities, seems . . . to have greatly hampered the social and economic development of China. Probably it is the complexity of her speech and writing, more than any other imaginable cause, that has made China to-day politically, socially, and individually a vast pool of backward people rather than the foremost power in the whole world.[1]

More than any other imaginable cause—the most unreconstructed McLuhanite could scarcely adopt a more uncompromising stance with respect to the power of technologies of communication to shape profoundly the cultures within which they operate.[2]

In fact, the confident diagnosis offered in the above passage constitutes a wholly representative moment within Wells's history of everything; it is a text informed by a thoroughgoing technological determinism, as well as an abiding belief in the tendency of communications technologies in particular to influence the essential character, and ultimate destiny, of imperial systems. Wells devotes much space to the emergence of various media, from alluvial clay and papyrus to submarine telegraph cables, usually in imperial contexts: in an early chapter focused on the empires of antiquity, each is typically introduced by a description including an account of its characteristic media, from Sumerian cuneiform and Egyptian hieroglyphics to the Peruvian *quipus,* while a subsequent chapter on writing systems reads rather like a roll-call of those same empires. Media often function for Wells as lenses for descrying the essence of a culture: he adduces, for example, a supposed resemblance between Mayan writing and the scribbling of European madmen in pronouncing the pre-Columbian civilizations to have been irrational, essentially "aberrant" (their "obsession" with bloodshed seems to follow as a matter of course from the unnatural "elaboration" of their script) (Wells, *Outline,* 194–95). But technologies of communication appear in more active roles as well: when Wells comes to discuss the European colonial enterprises of the modern era (China's loss is their gain), he credits, or blames, "the increased speed and certainty of transport and telegraphic communications," seemingly above all other factors, for their emergence (ibid., 1168). And the United States, in Wells's view, owes its (paradoxically) organic unity entirely to the nineteenth century's "new means of communication, the steamboat and railway and . . . electric telegraph" (ibid., 1131).[3] The Civil War, indeed, appears as a kind of ripple or glitch in the otherwise smooth evolution of networks: "At the beginning of the war there was no railway to the Pacific coast; now the railways spread like a swiftly growing plant until they had clutched and held and woven all the vast territories of the United States into one now indissoluble mental and material unity" (ibid., 1140–41).

But while the *Outline* was a text whose composition was avowedly spurred by the Great War, the crucible of such ideas should be sought earlier, at the end of the nineteenth century, the period during which Wells produced the pioneering fiction for which he is best remembered. The half-decade or so during which virtually all of Wells's enduring scientific romances appeared, in rapid succession (*The Time Machine* [1895], *The Island of Doctor Moreau* [1896], *The Invisible Man* [1897], *The War of the Worlds* [1898], *When the Sleeper Wakes* [1899], and *The First Men in the Moon* [1901]), as well as his first forays into the realm of cultural and social prophesy (particularly his 1901 *Anticipations*), saw the British Empire approaching its high-water mark; meanwhile, the evolution of modern media continued to accelerate (the cinema proper was developed, for instance, and the radio invented). As I will show, Wells drew heavily on the latter conceptual domain in framing his (largely critical) ideas about the former. Accordingly, I propose here to treat the fin-de-siècle writing of Wells as a particularly rich and striking example of the kind of conceptual interchange that is the subject of this book.

As I have already suggested, Wells had an enduring fascination with (as well as a singularly expansive conception of) communications technologies. The new media of the day figure prominently in his fiction, and elaborate blends and extrapolations of Victorian technologies fill his future worlds. Moreover, Wells was attuned to the potentialities inherent in a wide range of natural forces and energies, which he viewed as potential channels of communication and traffic.[4] (It is striking, indeed, how many of his classic novels are premised upon the exploitation, manipulation, or transformation of a particular such medium: gravity in *The First Men in the Moon*, time in *The Time Machine*, light in *The Invisible Man*, heat in *The War of the Worlds*.) Furthermore, the frequency with which Wells crafted figures of sensory amputation, isolation, and distortion, such as hypertrophied and atrophied sense-organs, suggests a particular concern with the contemporary deformation or renegotiation of the human sensorium. *The Invisible Man*, for instance, together with contemporaneous tales like "The Country of the

Blind," can be read as McLuhanesque parables of sensory imbalance in the unstable media ecologies of the fin de siècle. (It is also suggestive that Wells began work on this tale of vanishing flesh and blood mere months after Röntgen's discovery of X-rays was widely publicized, with photographs appearing showing the human body rendered all but invisible—Griffin's discovery merely takes the process to its logical conclusion.)

But above all, as I suggest above, media became crucially important to Wells's conceptualization of cultural, and particularly imperial, systems. They provided Wells with indispensable tools for thinking about empire, in both satires of contemporary imperialism like *The War of the Worlds* and *The First Men in the Moon* and his "prophetic" works from the same period, so often concerned with Britain's cultural survival in the future. In the first two texts, upon which I will primarily focus here, Wells elaborates monitory parables that link near-infinite imperial expansion with the threat of imperial extinction, using the imaginative possibilities he discerned in technologies of communication. In the latter works, media become core ingredients of a vision of the future that constitutes, I suggest, a transposition or displacement of his own imperialist impulses. By studying Wells's conceptual uses of media one can, I believe, learn much about how forms of imperial space and time were imagined at this moment in history. In so doing one may also be led to conclude that one of the most impressive accomplishments of such connective technologies may have inhered in their power to bind together what seem to us hopelessly contradictory, even paradoxical, ideological blends.

II.

When, in the aftermath of the Martians' first, deadly use of their "Heat Ray," the British Army are deployed to Woking, they bring with them, in addition to their field-guns and Maxims, a curious instrument "with a stand like a theodolite" (a surveying tool) (*War*, 58). The narrator has to be told that the unfamiliar object is a heliograph—also known as a "sun-telegraph"—a portable signaling device in the form of a tripod-mounted mirror, which uses reflected natural light to communicate in the field (widely used in the later nineteenth century until largely superannuated, its distinctive virtue of wirelessness mooted, by the new radio). Periodically the technology appears in the novel as an instrument of "warning" used by "devoted scouts" defending their homeland against the invader (ibid., 67) and, more symbolically, as a comforting emblem overhead. When the panicked curate asks the narrator, "What is that flicker in the sky?" he responds: "I told him that it was the heliograph signalling—that it was the sign of human help and effort in the sky" (ibid., 71).

This depiction of the heliograph in the hands of plucky rebels who are courageously, if seemingly futilely, trying to repel a powerful imperial force may uncannily anticipate its use by the underdog Boers *against* the English a few years later.[5] But it does not very comfortably square with its actual historical use by the British Empire during the few decades of its heyday. If the narrator of *The War of the Worlds* has never seen a heliograph before, it is for good reason: unlike, say, the telegraph (equally at home in Delhi or Birmingham), it was a technology overwhelmingly, if not solely, to be found in colonial contexts, in the service of projects of conquest and control. Its appearance on English soil in the novel would, then, have signaled to readers both the devastation of the domestic communications infrastructure and the fact that Albion had itself become a colonial space, the site of an imperial war of conquest, since the technology would have had fairly unambiguous resonances as a metonym of Empire. A look at the *Oxford English Dictionary's* entry on the heliograph is revealing. Of the eight citations given, all of which date from between 1877 and 1899, nearly all are taken from newspaper and magazine accounts of contemporary military actions (plus one Kipling story) which, taken together, form a kind of radically truncated, but fairly representative, chronicle of British imperialist activity during that period, from Burma to the Sudan, from the Second Anglo-Afghan War to the Boer War.[6] Other colonial and neocolonial powers were not slow to follow this lead: after "learn[ing] of British success in India," for instance, the US Army used the heliograph against the Apaches, to decisive effect (Sterling, *Military Communications*, 210). The technology was, then, in reality a rather unequivocally imperial medium, largely devoted to the work of subjugation and widely associated with the colonial wars of the later nineteenth century.

I want to suggest that the heliograph should be read as a less monstrous analogue of, or precursor to, the Martians' formidable Heat Ray itself—a weapon pointedly likened by Wells to "the parabolic mirror of a lighthouse," and mounted on a great ambulatory tripod (*War*, 27). Figuratively, at least, it is a signaling device transformed wholly into a devastating prosthesis of Empire. Just as Wells confronts Britons with a possible future incarnation of themselves in his Martians (a possibility he first explored in his "Man in the Year Million," a text referred to with comic obliquity within the novel), so does the Heat Ray represent the ultimate evolution of the "sun-telegraph," the medium used by British forces in Afghanistan, India, and Africa: its light become pure heat, a signal become pure weapon.

For a novel that has been long, and surely correctly, identified as a deliberate critique of nineteenth-century, particularly British, imperialism (with readers from Isaac Asimov to Stephen Arata seeing in the novel a parable of "reverse colonization"[7]), the British Empire is curiously absent from *The War of the Worlds*. There is, to be sure, the well-known reference to the "extermination" of Tasmanian aborigines in the first chapter, justly cited in such accounts (though even here "European immigrants," rather than Britons specifically, are indicted). But I find no direct mention of any British (or for that matter European) colony, with the exception of Ireland, afterwards in the text, nor of Britain's status as a global colonial power. This is surely because the British Empire is present in counterfactual form in the novel, externalized and symbolized as the Martians' invading force itself; England, in effect, is confronted with its own possible (imperial) future. I want to argue in what follows that technologies of communication and transport are central to the imperial critique contained within the novel. As my above reading of the Heat Ray suggests, these technologies contribute to such a critique in the first place by helping Wells to contrast two distinct models of political and social organization, reflected in their respective relationships to media. Just as the Martians' chief *weapon* is conceptually congruent with one of the later nineteenth century's more conspicuously "imperial" media, so do their uses of media themselves suggest their understanding of these as above all forms of imperial weaponry, instruments of conquest rather than aids to communication. From their telescopes to their transport cylinders (metaphorically likened to "missiles" fired from an interplanetary "gun") (*War*, 8, 6), Martian technologies of communication, transport, and perception are bent entirely towards the single end of colonial subjugation. At this historical juncture, of course, European powers were employing the telegraph, railway, and other technologies of communication in precisely this manner, as, again, the work of Daniel Headrick has shown. At the heart of British colonial supremacy was the use of media, among other technologies, as weapons. In Wells's novel, however, there is little, if any, sense of these imperial networks' existence at all (a strong indication, again, that the Martians' colonial enterprise itself represents an imaginative externalization of the British imperial project).

There is, moreover, a lesson to be discerned in the very morphology of the Martians, who have, in effect, themselves evolved into monstrous analogues of their own media, Spencerian blends of biological organism and radically centralized, radiate network. As Laura Otis has observed, the network metaphor was capable of alternately sustaining either the figure of imperial centralization or its less hierarchical opposite (*Networking*, 224–25). If the latter (as she has demonstrated) frequently underlay nineteenth-century figurations of the body, Wells, writing near the high-water mark of empire, imagines organisms grotesquely embodying the former. As biological analogues of what Otis calls the "centralized webs [that] 'wired' empires" (ibid., 225), the Martians are early literalizations of the cliché of the expansionist (for instance, imperialist or fascist) "octopus," a trope closely associated not only with military aggression but with sprawling webs of communication, with cables conceptualized as tentacles, grasping extensions of imperial power. The horrible bodies of the Martians, in other words, suggest a kind of cautionary just-so story for an imperial race: over time, Wells seems to say, we become our technologies, as well as the relationships they engender and embody.

By contrast, media technologies are conceptualized quite differently by Wells's Britons. The English, first of all, think of media as above all (at the risk of sounding tautological) a means of communication: of establishing contact, for instance, even with the (utterly) alien. There is accordingly a radical asymmetry in the exchanges between Britons and Martians, with the former trying to signal the latter, who respond in turn with bursts of unmeaning destruction. Where the Martians mean conquest, the naïve earthlings see attempts at communication. When the Martians first fire their cylinders at Earth, "the vulgar idea" is that these flashes constitute a "signal" (Wells, *War*, 7). And when the first cylinder with its occupants lands, the narrator's "mind [runs] fancifully on the possibilities of its containing manuscript, [and] on the difficulties in translation that might arise." In London the newspaper headlines read: "A MESSAGE RECEIVED FROM MARS." A "Deputation" subsequently "approach[es] them [the Martians] with signals, that we too were intelligent. . . . Flutter, flutter went the flag, first to the right, then to the left" (ibid., 23). The response is "a flash of light," bursts of green "smoke" or "flame," "the ghost of a beam of light," a series of "hissing," "humming," and "droning" noises, and bursts of invisible heat which issue from the cylinder: the semblance of communication, perhaps, but unparsed into significance, and bringing instant death (ibid., 24). Later "Fresh attempts [are] made to signal," but "The Martians took as much notice of such advances as we should take the lowing of a cow" (ibid., 39). The Martians, for their part, only talk to each other, their telepathic communication rather resembling the dedicated wires used as instruments of colonial control in British India, through whose channels Britons discussed the best ways to manage the natives.

Corresponding to this different conception of media on the part of the besieged British nation is a different performative function. Instead of instruments of subjugation, media serve as binding agents: as the novel makes abundantly clear, networks of communication knit the British social organism together. For Wells media literally "inform" societies, giving them shape and coherence. Among other things *The War of the Worlds* provides a panoramic snapshot of Western technologies of communication and transport by century's end, with newspapers, railways, telegraphs, and steamships all conspicuous presences in the narrative. And throughout the novel Wells presents a picture of a networked social and cultural totality, whose disintegration and subsequent reconstitution are repeatedly figured in terms of such technologies.

The devastation of England's networks is indeed one of the Martians' first tactical goals, as "They . . . cut every telegraph, and wrecked the railways" (ibid., 105).[8] Wells devotes much time to descriptions of the destroyed railways in particular: early in the novel, the last image the reader encounters before the Martians' landing is of "the brightness of the red, green, and yellow signal lights" of the railway, accompanied by the soothing, distant sounds of the trains themselves in the station, comforting indices of a "safe and tranquil" England (ibid., 9). After the first wave of destruction, the narrator, surveying the carnage from his study window, makes out a mangled train (its lamp still a "vivid glare" amid the wreckage) (ibid., 50) and a single "white railway signal," a lonely survivor of the railway's ruin (ibid., 54).[9] Telegraphic communications, too, dwindle and finally vanish, and London's busy, non-stop circulation of newspapers (the "fluttering" of "pink sheets") (ibid., 78) comes to a sudden end, the last editions printed in still-wet ink (a detail which, by foregrounding its material basis, perhaps prefigures the medium's imminent destruction). Wells later uses the same trope in a memorable image of the total dissolution of English social organization:

> Directly below him [a] balloonist would have seen the network of streets far and wide, houses, churches, squares, crescents, gardens . . . spread out like a huge map, and in the southward *blotted*. Over Ealing, Richmond, Wimbledon, it would have seemed as if some monstrous pen had flung ink upon the chart. Steadily, incessantly, each black splash grew and spread, shooting out ramifications this way and that, now banking itself against rising ground, now pouring swiftly over a crest into a new-found valley, exactly as a gout of ink would spread itself upon blotting-paper. (ibid., 105)

Where there had been an ordered space of circulating information, there is now a centrifugally expanding Rorschach blot; in its flight, the population of the metropolis is likened to the degree zero of mediality: raw matter without informing symbol.

The reconstitution of the English social organism is likewise figured in terms of the restoration of its communications networks, beginning with the telegraph:

One man—the first [to learn of the Martians' demise]—had gone to St Martin's-le-Grand, and . . . had contrived to telegraph to Paris. Thence the joyful news had flashed all over the world; a thousand cities, chilled by ghastly apprehensions, suddenly flashed into frantic illuminations; they knew of it in Dublin, Edinburgh, Manchester, Birmingham, at the time when I stood upon the verge of the pit. (ibid., 172)

In short order, the repair of the railway system follows, and the narrator buys a first copy of the *Daily Mail,* mostly "blank" and amateurishly produced by a "solitary compositor," as though, being newly reborn, the press must pass again through an embryonic phase (ibid., 174).

The treatment of the telegraph, however, is particularly revealing. Communications, notably, are limited to nonimperial channels (those extensive and vitally important networks linking colonial center and periphery, which may as well not exist in this novel), as aid arrives in copious flows from "Across the Channel, across the Irish Sea, across the Atlantic" (ibid., 172). Improbably, no colonial possession not bound by ties of language and/ or race is mentioned or even implied in the global reestablishment of telegraphic communications; the imperial reality of fin-de-siècle Britain remains largely occluded, or (again) transposed onto the Martians.[10] At the close of Wells's novel, the dominant trope is one of global community, a nascent version of Wells's "world-state," figured as a system of communication between and among interlocutors, rather than a system of exploitation modeled and abetted by cables extended from a controlling center. With the death of these cybernetic octopoi from the future, Britain's own imperial future is imaginatively exorcised, as the novel ends with the suggestion of a world without colonies, one in which England may perhaps yet avoid the fate of the tentacular imperialists from outer space.

The second respect in which such technologies seem indispensable to the novel's imperial critique involves Wells's figuration of forms of imperial space and time, specifically his delineation, in his scientific romances critical of empire, of the parameters of an imperial chronotope linking expansion and duration in a broadly inverse relationship. Indeed, the colonial venture of Wells's Martians nicely, even heuristically, exemplifies precisely such a dialectic. One who wanted to press Harold Innis's core thesis—introduced in the last chapter—to its limits might argue that it is their lack of a terrestrial evolutionary history (a genetically transmitted tradition or "memory" of conditions on earth) that dooms both the Martians and their flora. But quite obviously, the invaders' power is premised first of all upon the technological mastery of space, their expansionist project aided and abetted by a host of strongly spatially biased media and modes of transport. From the preternaturally powerful telescopes that permit them to study life on earth ("instruments . . . such as we have scarcely dreamed of" [ibid., 4]), to their transport cylinders, swift-striding tripods, and flying machines, the Martians employ implosive, spatially oriented technologies of conquest. However, their dominion is of course radically evanescent, as the invaders succumb, in a manner presaged by the fate of the aggressive, but ephemeral, "red weed" they have brought with them, to bacterial infection. The rise and fall of the Martian Empire is, therefore, ably contained within the narrative confines of a slim novel, rather than a chronicle of Gibbonian length. Their interplanetary adventure thus combines virtually infinite expansion in space with shockingly brief dominion in time. In its suggestion of an inverse relationship between expansion and duration (one, again, framed in terms of implosive technologies dragooned into the service of empire) the novel serves as a monitory parable in an age of (as Wells saw them) irresponsibly expansionist powers.

III.

In his search for absolute "solitude" (he intends to try his hand at playwriting after self-inflicted business losses), Bedford, the feckless narrator of *The First Men in the Moon,* settles on Lympne in Kent. This former port in Roman Britain is now choked off from contact with the sea and bordered by stretches of nearly impassable clay, reduced thereby from a prominent node within an imperial network to a merely picturesque congeries of imperial relics, in the form of scattered Roman ruins. (And Lympne's inhospitality, as well as comparative irrelevance, to modern networks of communication also is suggested by the figure of a lone postman struggling to negotiate the local mud with boards strapped to his feet.) A note of imperial evanescence and decay is thus sounded almost immediately within the novel, in a passage that establishes an intimate connection between empires and the channels of traffic and communication that sustain them:

> I doubt if the place would be there at all, if it were not a fading memory of things gone for ever. It was the big port of England in Roman times, Portus Lemanis, and now the sea is four miles away. . . . I used to stand on the hill and think of it all, the galleys and legions, the captives and officials, the women and traders, the speculators like myself, all the swarm and tumult that came clanking in and out of the harbour. . . . And where the port had been were the levels of the marsh . . . dotted here and there with tree

clumps and the church towers of old mediæval towns that are following Lemanis now towards extinction. (Wells, *First Men*, 7)

The imperial center of gravity has of course shifted, in the intervening centuries, from Rome (the ultimate expansionist empire of antiquity) to former satellites like Britain. The channels of imperial traffic have expanded as well: Britain's own dominion over the seas had, for instance, by century's end come not only to appropriate the power of steam[11] but also to incorporate the ocean's depths, as well as its surfaces.[12] And in its figuration of gravity, technologically harnessed for the purposes of transit, as *itself* a means of potential colonial exploitation, the novel seems to suggest not only the dependence of empires upon such channels but also the truth that these will continue to evolve in as-yet-unknowable ways: a point hammered home by the prominent place Wells accords the new wireless in his colonialist parable of the new century. There are a number of continuities between *The First Men in the Moon* and *The War of the Worlds* with respect to their treatment of media. Once again, for instance, they are used as differentiating markers, tropes suggesting the profound cultural differences between the two civilizations—(would-be) colonizer and colonized, respectively—that are brought into contact within the novel.[13] And once again, technologies of communication are central to the construction of an imperial chronotope linking colonial expansion with cultural fragility.

As many have remarked, *The First Men in the Moon*, published in 1901 and serialized during the Boer War (which is referenced by Cavor in his discourse with an increasingly uneasy Grand Lunar), functions on one level, and fairly conspicuously, as a critique of, or comment upon, contemporary European, particularly British, imperialism. It is a kind of parable about the potential conquest and exploitation of the greatest satellite known to us. Upon their arrival on the moon (in one well-known episode), Bedford and Cavor soon find themselves weak with hunger, and decide to try some local fungi that, unfortunately, have powerfully intoxicating properties. Bedford's mind, divested of inhibition, immediately begins to run on imperial possibilities, "projects of colonisation": "We must annex this moon," he begins to babble drunkenly. "This is part of the White Man's Burthen. Cavor—we are—*hic*—Satap—mean Satraps! Nempire Cæsar never dreamt. B'in all the newspapers. Cavorecia. Bedfordecia. Bedfordecia—*hic*—Limited. Mean— unlimited! Practically" (*First Men*, 82). As David Lake, who calls the novel an "anti-imperialist satire," points out:

This satire would have been intensely topical in 1900–01. 'Cavorecia' and 'Bedfordecia' are clear parodies of 'Rhodesia,' the name bestowed in 1895

on the territories in southern Africa seized by the imperialist tycoon Cecil
Rhodes and his associates. . . . (Introduction, xxv)

Numerous parallels between Wells's moon and southern Africa may be
established, and I will not belabor them here, other than to suggest that it
is probably no accident that Bedford perceives "kopjes" on the lunar surface, or that the hollow, inhabited moon constitutes a literalization of the
predominant conceptual metaphor of Africa as having an "exterior" and an
"interior," a kind of shell to be penetrated. The figure of verticality also calls
to mind the obsessive mining for gold and diamonds whose discovery had
awakened Britain's interest in its neglected African possessions in the first
place: Wells imagines the moon as a space shot through with great holes
and deep shafts, a land with tunnels studded with crystals which "scintil-
lated like gems" (*First Men,* 103), and "gold as common as iron or wood"
(ibid., 197). The connection with mining may explain, too, Wells's decision
to limn the moon's lucre-crammed interior with a pervasive blue phospho-
rescence, since prospecting by men like Rhodes had revealed the existence,
deep below the surface, of a diamond-rich "blue earth," which soon became
idiomatic. Rhodes is reported to have remarked upon "the power that this
blue ground would confer on the man who obtained control of it all" (Brendon, *Decline,* 194).

But the link in Wells's mind between his protagonists and men like
Rhodes (made all but explicit in the passage quoted above) suggests a further
affinity, one of particular salience in the present context: namely, the association between expansionist projects and powerfully spatially biased technologies. Perhaps the most iconic image of Rhodes in British popular culture is,
of course, the *Punch* cartoon ("The Rhodes Colossus") which depicts "the
visionary of British expansion" (ibid.) straddling Africa with extended arms.
(Perhaps Wells had this famous image in mind when he envisioned Bedford
and Cavor making their immense, low-gravity bounds from a "lichenous
kopje"—they do seem rather like pygmified Rhodeses as they take their "gargantuan strides" across the lunar landscape [Wells, *First Men,* 67–68].) What
is less often remarked is the fact that those arms are stringing an impossi-
bly long telegraph wire across the length of the continent. The image is, in
other words, at the same time a reflection of Rhodes's preoccupation with the
nineteenth century's paradigmatic territory-extending and -binding technologies, the telegraph and railway: a preoccupation exemplified in his dream of a
"Cape to Cairo" network. Like Rhodes and other colonialists of the period,[14]
Wells's protagonists are associated with the mastery of powerful spatially
oriented media—crucially, the technological exploitation of gravity which
enables their lunar voyage in the first place, and Cavor's later use of the new

technology of radio to send messages back to the earth from the moon (after he has taken advantage of the Selenites' trusting nature in building an improvised transmitter).

These two forces, I would suggest, function in the text as figures for the new media of the day (with gravity serving as an imaginative extrapolation of those of the future), as well as their probable recruitment by capitalist and imperialist projects. Bedford unequivocally views Cavor's technological harnessing of gravity as a new means of colonialist exploitation, enabling one-way flows of purloined wealth from satellite to center (with "guns," predictably, going in the other direction) (ibid., 118). According to the scientific logic of the novel, these forces are rigorously continuous, as the theoretical basis of Cavor's discovery inheres in Wells's inclusion of gravity within the great family of electromagnetic energies. In Cavor's gloss, gravity is explicitly affiliated with both X-rays and radio waves—again, two of the most spectacular scientific discoveries of the previous decade:

> "Radiant energy," he [Cavor] made me [Bedford] understand, was anything like light or heat, or those Röntgen Rays there was so much talk about a year or so ago, or the electric waves of Marconi, or gravitation. All these things, he said, *radiate* out from centres, and act on bodies at a distance, whence comes the term "radiant energy." (ibid., 16)

There is thus a certain Maxwellian symmetry informing the novel's structure: gravity "waves" are used to transmit English bodies to the moon, and radio waves to transmit English words back again.

But while Bedford's visions of conquest bristle with boundless imperialist confidence, Cavor's wireless transmissions, which dominate the last fifth or so of the novel, suggest a far less sanguine image of British expansion. Wells's treatment of the radio, indeed, powerfully depicts the reverse of the expansionist medal: namely, the fact that the fantasy of "practically" "unlimited" (in Bedford's phraseology) spatial dominion was always haunted by fears of cultural dispersion, evanescence, and fragmentation. Cavor's communications are interspersed with commentary and, at times, interpretation by Bedford, necessary because of the extremely problematic nature of these messages as they are received on Earth (where they are recorded by phonograph, subsequently to be transcribed as writing). Bedford comments at some length upon the "curiously fragmentary message[s]" picked up by a "Dutch electrician" following in Tesla's footsteps by pointing his radio equipment skyward—and particularly upon the factors contributing to this fragmentation. "Unhappily," he muses, "they are only fragments, and the most momentous of all the things that he had to tell humanity . . . have throbbed themselves away unrecorded into space" (ibid., 173). He goes on to adduce a host of further reasons for the messages' frustrating incompleteness, complaining that Cavor's "communication comes and goes in our records in an extremely fitful manner; it becomes blurred; it 'fades out' in a mysterious and altogether exasperating way. . . . Altogether we have probably lost quite half of the communications he made, and much we have is damaged, broken, and partly effaced. In the abstract that follows the reader must be prepared therefore for a considerable amount of break, hiatus, and change of topic" (ibid., 173–74). To the high degree of ellipsis and semantic indeterminacy is added a considerable amount of redundancy, a fact which gives Bedford license to edit and shape the transmissions: "The messages of Cavor . . . are for the most part so much broken, and they abound so in repetitions, that they scarcely form a consecutive narrative" (ibid., 182).

It is worth noting that Bedford's laments first of all reflect a pervasive association, in the early days of wireless, of loss, dispersion, and entropic waste with the very concept of "broadcasting" signals, as opposed to sending them directly from point A to point B: "In 1899 . . . *The Electrician* contended that 'messages scattered broadcast only waste energy by travelling with futile persistence toward celestial space'" (Briggs and Burke, *Social History,* 155). As Thomas Richards suggests, in his reading of *Tono-Bungay,* Wells was perhaps uniquely attuned, among his contemporaries, to the emergent theme of entropy (*Imperial Archive,* 88). In Cavor's disintegrating, noise-troubled broadcasts, I want to suggest, he uses this figure to craft a compelling tableau depicting cultural dispersion, perhaps annihilation.

Eventually (after the Selenites become aware, through the graphic descriptions of the ingenuously garrulous Cavor, of the bellicose habits of mankind) his transmissions are further garbled by the deliberate interference of the lunar natives, in the form of electromagnetic sabotage:

> At this point a series of undulations . . . become confusingly predominant in the record . . . curiously suggestive of some operator deliberately seeking to mix them in with his message and render it illegible. . . . For a long time nothing can be made of this madly zigzagging trace; then quite abruptly the interruption ceases, leaves a few words clear, and then resumes . . . completely obliterating whatever Cavor was attempting to transmit. (Wells, *First Men,* 211)

This surreptitious work of effacement, the intentional blending of signal with noise, is ultimately succeeded (in Bedford's imagination at least) by physical assault, as Cavor is dragged bodily from his apparatus even as he is attempting to transmit the secret of making "Cavorite" back home:

> And then suddenly, like a cry in the night, like a cry that is followed by a stillness, came the last message. It is the briefest fragment, the broken beginnings of two sentences.
>
> The first was: "I was mad to let the Grand Lunar know—"
>
> There was an interval of perhaps a minute. One imagines some interruption from without. A departure from the instrument—a dreadful hesitation among the looming masses of apparatus in that dim, blue-lit cavern—a sudden rush back to it, full of a resolve that came too late. Then, as if it were hastily transmitted, came: "Cavorite made as follows: take—"
>
> There followed one word, a quite unmeaning word as it stands: "uless."
>
> And that is all.
>
> It may be he made a hasty attempt to spell "useless" when his fate was close upon him. Whatever it was that was happening about that apparatus we cannot tell. Whatever it was we shall never, I know, receive another message from the moon. For my own part a vivid dream has come to my help, and I see . . . Cavor struggling in the grip of these insect Selenites, struggling ever more desperately and hopelessly as they press upon him, shouting, expostulating, perhaps even at last even fighting, and being forced backward step by step out of all speech or sign of his fellows, for evermore into the Unknown—into the dark, into that silence that has no end. . . . (ibid., 213)

This tableau, consciously or not, rather strikingly echoes the telegraph-office episode from the Indian Mutiny, discussed in chapter one. But the focus in these final scenes on linguistic fragmentation and loss, followed by radical indeterminacy (Cavor's broadcast ends on a note of perpetual entropic suspension, with the "quite unmeaning" "uless") and finally, a radio silence that figures death, resonates with particular force when read in the context of Wells's imperial dialectic of space and time.

Prosaically, of course, Wells's emphasis on the fragmentary character of Cavor's lunar transmissions serves the needs of his plot, by explaining why the secret of Cavorite must remain forever unknown. But it also contributes to a powerful final image of Cavor's (English) words traveling near-infinite distances in space, while suffering a corresponding loss of integrity and coherency (including mutilation by native resistance), before finally vanishing altogether. Englishness (with language serving, as so often, as a cultural or racial stand-in) has overextended itself, and flies broadcast, scattered and distorted, across infinite space, destroying itself in the process. It is not difficult to detect a note of warning to an expansionist nation in this media-inspired trope of dispersion and evanescence: the novel, which began with fragments of imperial Roman culture embedded in the clay of vanished seas, ends with fragments of English words graven in the wax of a revolving cylinder: "This intermittent trickle of messages, this whispering of a record needle" (ibid., 197), giving way at last to silence.

IV.

The trope of damaged communication takes on a similar note of urgency in Wells's more temporally focused, "prophetic" texts from the same period (both fictional and nonfictional), in the form of the specter of noise introduced into historical, hereditary, and evolutionary narratives. There is accordingly in these texts a contrapuntal emphasis placed on what Innis would call time-biased media. Most famously, of course, in *The Time Machine* Wells imagines temporality as itself a medium of transmission, the Time Traveller's vehicle being precisely analogous to the ship implied by the title of the tale's original incarnation ("The Chronic Argonauts"), as well as the manned balloons adduced by the Traveller in his heuristic discussion of the essential continuity of space and time. It is indeed upon this story's core, proleptically Einsteinian premise—that "duration" is in fact a form or mode of "extension," rather than its facile opposite—that Wells would erect the imaginative superstructure of his own transposed imperial fantasies. He envisioned, in other words, empires of time *and* space, of temporal as well as territorial extension, in contradistinction to the rapidly expanding but evanescent bubbles represented, in his view, by the colonial projects of the nineteenth century.

Once again, the new communications technologies of the day provided Wells with essential conceptual material for imagining the possible forms of such futures, as he explored the problems of dissemination—cultural, linguistic, and racial—over time, and with the role media might play as agents or models of such transmissions. In two loosely connected fictions, for instance, set two centuries in the future—*When the Sleeper Wakes* (1899) and *A Story of the Days to Come* (1897/1899)—much attention is given to the media of that future, and particularly to their role in preserving, or shaping, British culture in the year 2100. In *Sleeper*, for instance, the eponymous sleeper Graham comes to consciousness in a future society in which English has become, for the underclasses at least, a corrupted, fragmentary "Pigeon" (*sic*) language, a tissue of "blurred and mangled distortions" confounding the interpretive powers of the bewildered, Victorian protagonist (Wells, *Sleeper,* 78). It is only "phonograph culture," the exposure of the privileged classes to stored linguistic paradigms, that has allowed for the survival of the narrative's own brand of "pure" (e.g. late Victorian, middle-class) English. As I discussed in chapter two, the "Edison era" saw the emergence of a host of "new inscriptive forms" such as the phonograph and kinematograph (Gitelman, *Scripts, Grooves, and Writing Machines,* 11). In Wells's fictions of the future, these new media of inscription appear prominently, often in novel, blended configurations such as "kineto-tele-photographs" and "kinematograph-phonographs." They are both culturally central (like the ubiquitous "Babble Machines" in *Sleeper*) and conspicuously involved in the active culture of the "race," associated with the reconstruction or reproduction of Englishness in the face of distortion, mutation, or amalgamation with the "alien." Upon encountering what seems to him a survival of the classic English "type" ("bluff" and "manly"), Graham is told that this ideal Briton has patterned himself after "phonographs and kinematographs"; he is, in other words, the product of late Victorian media premised upon the capture of voice and movement (Wells, *Sleeper,* 105).

These inscriptive media constitute a temporal counterpart to the radically space-biased technologies so prominently featured in the imperial parables from the same period, offering the promise of new capacities for the preservation of information, in new modalities—the spoken word, the moving image. They thus held out the possibility, ostensibly at least, for cultural, and by extension racial, preservation across vast spans of time, at a historical moment at which such questions of survival loomed large in the British imagination. Yet at the same time these texts suggest the essentially quixotic nature of the attempt to freeze cultural forms, like linguistic paradigms, in time, to transmit the signs of Englishness unblemished into the future. The treatment of the new media of inscription within these texts suggests the folly of such an archival logic, given the kinetic dispensation of evolutionary time, the ineluctable realities of linguistic and cultural drift. When, for example, the newly awakened Graham explores the gilded cage to which he has been forcibly conveyed, he soon notices the absence of written texts, discovering in their stead "the latter-day substitute[s] for [the] novel"—"peculiar double cylinders" like videotapes, on which are recorded filmed versions of stories, to be played on a television-like box. Among the library of stored narratives he finds three tales the contemporary reader would have recognized. Their labels, however, are at first blush profoundly confusing:

The lettering on the cylinders puzzled him. At first sight it seemed like Russian. Then he noticed a suggestion of mutilated English about certain of the words.

"Ɵi Man huwdbi Kiŋ,"

forced itself on him as "The Man who would be King." "Phonetic spelling," he said. He remembered reading a story with that title, then he recalled the story vividly, one of the best stories in the world. . . . He puzzled out the titles of two adjacent cylinders. "The Heart of Darkness," he had never heard of before nor "The Madonna of the Future"—no doubt if they were indeed stories, they were by post Victorian [sic] authors. (Wells, Sleeper, 39)

The trope of phonetic writing functions similarly in A Story of the Days to Come, which depicts a postliterate England (similarly full of kinematographs and phonographs), which has ostensibly arrested linguistic drift, at least in its privileged classes:

In spite of the intervening space of time, the English language was almost exactly the same as it had been in England under Victoria the Good. The invention of the phonograph and suchlike means of recording sound, and the gradual replacement of books by such contrivances, had . . . arrested the process of change in accent that had hitherto been so inevitable. (Wells, Story, 195)

Yet this statement is trenchantly undermined for the reader by the defamiliar-izing effect of such spellings as "Mwres" for "Morris," "Elizebeɵ" for "Eliza-beth," and "'ETS" for "hats"; markers of difference which mirror the larger changes time and technology have wrought in this rather dystopian future. (In the lower classes, without access to these technologies, language drift has proceeded apace, nearly to the point of unintelligibility.)

What alternatives did Wells envision? A world without difference—the antithesis of the diverse British Empire as he would characterize it in the Outline, and a world that, in his view, modern technologies of acceleration, with their power to compress time and space alike (in the Victorian cliché, to "annihilate" both), made tantalizingly possible. As Carolyn Marvin points out, fantasies abounded in the late nineteenth century of global networks that would annihilate not only space and time but difference; she discusses, for instance, an 1893 story by Julian Hawthorne that imagines future "communi-ties of homogeneous culture, race, [and] language" (Marvin, When Old Tech-nologies Were New, 201). Wells's bestselling Anticipations develops the same themes in (disconcertingly earnest) nonfictional form. Subtitled "the Reaction of Mechanical and Scientific Progress Upon Human Life and Thought," it begins with a discussion of "means of communication" and "methods of transit," as Wells paints a picture of global technological diffusion focusing upon networks of transit and telephony. In his first chapter, for instance, Wells asserts the historical autonomy of "the evolution of locomotion" as a historical determinant, noting that "upon transport, upon locomotion, may . . . hang the most momentous issues of politics and war" (*Anticipations,* 2). But perhaps the crucial medium in *Anticipations* proves to be language itself, which Wells envisioned as above all "an instrument of world unification" (Mattelart, *Invention,* 192), projecting what he saw as trends of linguistic, and accordingly cultural, homogenization forward to conjure up a vision of a networked world dominated by a single tongue. Wells predicted a future battle royal between English and French (with a few dark horses in the race) for global hegemony. He imagined a process of global homogenization beginning with the "arrest" of linguistic "differentiation" through "unifying" technologies (he writes of "a whole wonderland of novel, space-destroying appliances") (Wells, *Anticipations,* 127).

But this is only prelude to his "New Republic," the "world-state" of "kinetic men" which, in the text's infamous conclusion,[15] will oversee the extinction of "the people of the abyss" (ibid., 177–78). Wells's "kinetic society," with its focus on accelerated flows of social circulation within ever-expanding networks, as well as the technological compression of temporality, resembles Paul Virilio's "dromocratic society" in many respects. In his "Essay on Dromology" (a term denoting a new theoretics of speed) Virilio anticipates that

> [w]ith the realization of dromocratic-type progress, humanity will stop being diverse. It will tend to divide only into *hopeful populations* (who are allowed the hope that they will reach, in the future, someday, the speed that they are accumulating . . .) and *despairing populations,* blocked by the inferiority of their technological vehicles, living and subsisting in a finite world. (*Speed and Politics,* 47, emphasis original)

This prophesied eradication of diversity, which is to be replaced by a binary schema of dromological haves and have-nots, can be mapped without much difficulty (albeit with a very different distribution of authorial sympathies) onto the Wellsian vision, with its "kinetic men" shadowed by the swarming "people of the abyss" described in *Anticipations,* and figured in various guises in his fictions of the future. There are, to be sure, vital differences between the two visions. I draw the parallel in order to suggest that, in elaborating an essentially imperial dromology, Wells here conjures with a conception of space and time different in crucial respects from those informing his anti-imperial romances of the same period.

For what, surely, is particularly likely to strike the modern reader is the perplexing lack of dissonance Wells perceived between these two simultaneously cultivated visions, between, on the one hand, his principled opposition to contemporary imperialism and, on the other, his enthusiastic advocacy of technologically saturated utopias premised upon the eradication of all difference. How, one wants to ask, did Wells reconcile such seemingly contradictory positions? In effect, by seeking a technological solution to an ideological problem: as a reading of texts like *Anticipations* shows, in writing about imperial systems Wells lets his technologically inflected chronotopes do much of his thinking for him. I have already discussed Menke's identification of a telegraphic chronotope in the age of realism. Of course, such tropes of infinite connectivity can—as I noted in chapter one—become highly problematic when applied to imperial contexts.[16] Fortunately, media environments (particularly, one suspects, emergent or evolving ones) provide material for envisioning a multiplicity of such spatial and temporal relationships. For example, in his *Charles Dickens in Cyberspace* (2003), Jay Clayton compellingly explores the importance of information technologies to the imaginative conception of the dispensation he terms "genome time" (whose ancestry he speculatively traces to Wells, in *The Time Machine*) (176). And as his writing of this crucial period clearly shows, Wells was capable of deriving multiple imperial chronotopes from media ecologies, conceptual tools which quite literally helped him to think the often contradictory thought of the age of empire.

Menke notes a long-standing indictment against media technologies, namely, the claim that they "[paper] over the epistemological gaps between representation and reality" (*Telegraphic Realism,* 248).[17] As the case of Wells shows, they can have the power to paper over, however imperfectly, ideological fissures as well; and few moments in modern history, perhaps, provide better examples of such fissiparousness than the age of imperialism.

CHAPTER FOUR

IMPERIAL INFORMATICS

I.

In John Buchan's spy thriller *Greenmantle* (1916), Buchan's hero, Richard Hannay, twice escapes the clutches of the hulking, fanatical Colonel von Stumm: first in the very heart of the German Empire, then on the outer fringes of its influence, at the Russo-Turkish border. On this second occasion Hannay manages to "burgl[e] old Stumm's private cabinet" as well (Buchan, *Greenmantle*, 213), making away with an annotated map of the Turkish defenses of Erzerum (i.e., Erzurum), spelling out their Achilles' heel with great explicitness. It offers in effect a set of instructions for a Russian victory, being now only "information confined to the Turkish and German staff. But if it could be conveyed to the Grand Duke he would have Erzerum in his power in a day" (ibid., 218). The search for some means of "conveyance" for this information promptly takes hold of Hannay's mind: in a "fever," he "long[s] for wireless, a carrier pigeon, an aeroplane—anything to bridge over that space of half a dozen miles between me and the Russian lines" (ibid.). He then realizes that he is already in possession of a *human* medium for the transference of the information, in the shape of the faithful Dutchman Peter Pienaar, who had distinguished himself by his "intelligence work in the Boer War" some fifteen years earlier (ibid., 220). Pienaar instantly recognizes the value of the information and realizes that he is the man for the job. But his function in the scene seems first of all to be to contextualize the task at hand in relation to an episode he recalls from the earlier (colonial) war, which is offered as a kind of conceptual frame or template, cast in fabular terms:

> "That news is worth many a million pounds," said he, wrinkling his brows, and scratching delicately the tip of his left ear. It was a way he had when he was startled.
>
> "How can we get it to our friends?"
>
> Peter cogitated. "There is but one way. A man must take it. Once, I remember, when we fought the Matabele it was necessary to find out whether the chief Makapan was living. Some said he had died, others that he'd gone over the Portuguese border, but I believed he lived. No native could tell us, and since his kraal was well defended no runner could get through. So it was necessary to send a man."
>
> Peter lifted up his head and laughed. "The man found the chief Makapan. He was very much alive, and made good shooting with a shot-gun. But the man brought the chief Makapan out of his kraal and handed him over to the Mounted Police. You remember Captain Arcoll, Dick—Jim Arcoll? Well, Jim laughed so much that he broke open a wound in his head, and had to have a doctor."
>
> "You were that man, Peter," I said.
>
> "Ja. I was the man. There are more ways of getting into kraals than there are ways of keeping people out." (ibid., 220–21)

There is a "black box" element to this tale ("Imagine a kraal which cannot be seen into. Inside there is, or is not, a living chief . . . "), suggesting a certain kinship with the genre of the modern thought experiment. Pienaar's narrative bears, for instance, at least a superficial resemblance to Schrödinger's famous story about a not dissimilarly situated cat. (Pienaar's tale has a less intellectually perplexing dénouement, if one at least as morally problematic.) At the same time, this seeming digression reads like a heuristic parable, offering an exemplary case in support of an ostensibly axiomatic truism, here about the nature of information ("There are more ways of getting into kraals than there are ways of keeping people out"). However, I propose to read Pienaar's colonial fable as a just-so story as well, a sort of zero-degree myth about the origin of information itself, as a distinctively modern conceptual entity.

The meaning of "information" has, of course, undergone significant, not to say radical, changes since its first appearance in the language. Etymologically suggestive of a process of shaping or stereotyping—of imprinting "forms" upon (paradigmatically) human minds—it has migrated from early associations with the language of legal complaint to become a ubiquitous syn-onym for such terms as "knowledge," "intelligence" and "news." More recently it has acquired something like an antithetical significance, as "a mathemati-cally defined quantity divorced from any concept of news or meaning" (*OED*)—the "information," that is, of "information theory" and "information science." And in this modern—or postmodern—incarnation, information is almost invariably associated with the Second World War. As the story goes, from that conflict emerged not only the A-bomb but also the modern con-cept of information: both that peculiar, rigorously quantifiable entity so use-ful to engineers and, in its wake, its own popular analogue—the ubiquitous, fetishized quantity from which so many viral phrases have sprouted, such as "the information society," "the information age," Virilio's "information bomb," and so on. It is certainly true, to be sure, that the particular scientific disci-pline known as information *theory* arose directly (though not entirely without precedents) from the "ferment of scientific activity" associated with World War II (Campbell, *Grammatical Man,* 11). It is not surprising, then, that his-torical accounts of information theory tend to invoke a familiar sequence of tableaux, set against a wartime backdrop and starring a pantheon of cyber-heroes *avant la lettre,* fighting the Axis powers with their brains: there is, for example, Norbert Wiener, ruminating the science of cybernetics into being while dreaming up more effective ways to shoot down Luftwaffe pilots; Alan Turing, along with his Bletchley Park colleagues, breaking the Nazis' Enigma cipher with their ticking, bomb-like computers; and Claude Shan-non, whose work on both of these species of military problem—ballistic and cryptographic—culminated in his postwar publication, with Warren Weaver, of the groundbreaking *Mathematical Theory of Communication,* the book that brought the "bit" into the world as a metric for information.[1] One recent account of information theory goes so far as to declare, "World War II was the first information war" (Seife, *Decoding the Universe,* 5–6).

As a reading of Buchan shows, however, the *First* World War was not only very much an "information war" as well, reliant like no earlier conflict upon information technologies, cryptographic techniques, and the like,[2] but also (and largely for this reason) a war during which it became possible to think in recognizably modern ways about information. I would, again, offer Peter Pienaar's tale of the sealed kraal (which is echoed by other episodes in Buchan) as one example, dramatizing as it does what one tends to think of as a later twentieth-century conceptualization, within a novel of the Great War (and giving it an even earlier, Boer War pedigree). Pienaar's mission has, in information-theory terms, a kind of severe purity: he is to acquire, as Shan-non would express it a world war later, a single, discrete bit of maximally consequential information, without which the local forces of empire must remain in an uneasy limbo of radical uncertainty.[3]

But equally striking, surely, is the context in which the parable unfolds: it is of course not only a story about information retrieval, but one about the exercise of imperial power as well. Accordingly, I want to argue in this chapter that Buchan's writing (which spanned several genres over the course of his career, from fiction to biography and history) is evidence of both a life-long imaginative engagement with a historically emergent conceptualization of information, and an equally enduring habit of using information to think about imperial systems.

Certainly empire and imperialism were central themes in the writing and thought of Buchan, who traveled to South Africa in his twenties to throw himself enthusiastically into the work of colonial reconstruction and died, four decades later, the Governor-General of Canada. One school of inter-pretation, indeed, sees his elevation of "the imperial idea" to the level of a quasi-religious belief system as something like the touchstone of his career: "Investing empire with an altogether ecclesiastical significance he looked on it as a God-given means whereby man in his secular condition could be inte-grated with his spiritual ideal" (Sandison, *Wheel of Empire,* 149). "Imperial-ism," on this view, was to be for Buchan "a unifying faith for the whole nation" (Kruse, *John Buchan,* 78). My contention here is that this imperial idea, or ideal, would have looked radically, even unrecognizably, different without its powerful inflection by the master trope of information.

By focusing on this aspect of Buchan's work and thought I do mean to assert, at least implicitly, that he was in some sense an exemplary or rep-resentative figure, giving voice to conceptual connections that were taking shape in his era. Yet it cannot be denied that he was more or less uniquely positioned in relation not only to the unfolding of what would prove to be the final chapter of Britain's imperial history but also to the modern his-tory of information itself. Buchan's most obvious connection with the latter lies, no doubt, in his own personal immersion in the world of propaganda and intelligence work during the Great War. Buchan played a prominent part in the creation and development of Britain's early information agen-cies, from his participation in the War Propaganda Bureau to his leadership of the first Department of Information, his position as Director of Intelli-gence, and subsequent role in the new Ministry of Information (Lownie, *John Buchan,* 125–34) (to say nothing of his own writing during this period, which included his popular *A History of the Great War* [1922], a text itself "easily, if wrongly, typecast as nationalist, patriotic propaganda" [Strachan, "John Buchan," 302]). This important aspect of Buchan's career, long neglected, has begun to attract increased attention in recent years: the prominent World War I historian Hew Strachan has written an illuminating essay exploring "the [wartime] relationship between Buchan the man of affairs, historian, and propagandist, and Buchan the novelist" (ibid., 304), while Ahmed al-Rawi considers Buchan's career as propagandist in relation to what he sees as the "Orientalism" of *Greenmantle* (al-Rawi, "Buchan the Orientalist," 1). Certainly, given Buchan's relationship with such institutions, it is hardly surprising that the fashioning and control of information and misinformation should constitute central themes in his novels, particularly those depicting the struggle of imperial rivals.

It is important to note, however, that even before the war Buchan was disposed to view imperial systems through the lens of a system of thought which privileged the realm of ideas as a primary, and shaping, force. For Buchan, as I will show, information was always the ally of order—and order, in his essentially Platonic worldview, was always something to be imposed from above, as ideational forms stamped upon matter. This basic conceptual frame served as the foundation, I argue, for all of Buchan's subsequent experiences with information—which, for him, would always be at bottom the form-giving entity implied by the word's etymology, a potent force for imposing order as well as a means of disseminating knowledge. In some respects idiosyncratic, in others culturally representative, Buchan's conception of information—its nature, value, and potential dangers—thus continued to evolve throughout his career, but always in an ongoing creative symbiosis with his ideas about empire.

In what follows, then, I propose to trace this process of evolution and its embodiment in Buchan's writings about the nature and future of imperialism. I begin by considering Buchan's early experiences in South Africa, which subsequently formed the basis of bestselling books of both fiction (*Prester John*) and nonfiction (*The African Colony*), works which resort to a technologically derived idiom of coding in their depiction of the challenges, and potential dangers, Britain faced in its future relationship with the native population. I then turn to a trio of important spy thrillers, all featuring Buchan's recurrent protagonist Richard Hannay ("precursor to Ian Fleming's James Bond" [Weintraub, "John Buchan Reassessed," 372]) and written during or in the aftermath of the Great War: *Greenmantle, Mr Standfast,* and *The Three Hostages.* In these texts the increasingly culturally central, and conceptually fluid, idea of information is given flesh, powerfully inflecting Buchan's imagination of a succession of threats to Britain's imperial hegemony, as well as its imperial champion.

II.

A few years before his death, Buchan completed a biography, "begun many years ago" (*Augustus,* 7), of Rome's first emperor. It is not difficult to discern the numerous parallels that Lord Tweedsmuir (as he then was) seems to have perceived between himself and his Julio-Claudian subject. Even at the intimate level of somatic experience, Buchan repeatedly refers to an incapacitating stomach ailment very like the one from which he himself suffered (and which he had also given to the American Blenkiron in the Richard Hannay novels).[4] There are also numerous references to Augustus as a master of propaganda and information control—work that as emperor he would farm out to figures like Maecenas ("his minister of propaganda" [ibid., 161–62) and Horace ("a vigorous propagandist" [ibid., 225]). But it is their shared experience as statesmen and administrators within an imperial system to which Buchan himself calls the most explicit attention. In his preface, he remarks that "since my undergraduate days Augustus has inspired me with a lively interest, which has been sustained by such experience as I have had, under varied conditions, of those problems of government which are much the same in every age" (ibid., 7). Given that the biography had been completed during the first "[t]wo Canadian winters" of his Governor-Generalship of that country (the preface is conspicuously signed "J. B., Government House, Ottawa" [ibid., 9]), its readers' first thoughts may well have been of Buchan's most recent term of colonial service. However, the book's treatment of Augustus owes much, I would suggest, to Buchan's early participation in the work of imperial administration many years before in Southern Africa, where as a bright young member of Lord Milner's so-called "Kindergarten" he had been directly involved in the project of colonial reconstruction undertaken in the aftermath of the Boer War.

That Buchan intends a close and sustained parallel with the British imperial experience is obvious. More than once, indeed, Buchan makes the parallel explicit, as when he observes that Augustus' "problem [in stabilizing the imperial borders] was that of Britain on the north-west border of India" (ibid., 303). And when he writes, "The extension of her [Rome's] boundaries had been achieved rather by accident than by design, for it was her desire to be secure in Italy that had forced an empire into her reluctant hands" (ibid., 26), few readers, surely, would have failed to hear echoes of Seeley's famous phrase about "conquer[ing] half the world in a fit of absence of mind" (Seeley, *Expansion of England,* 10) ringing in the background. But the parallels between the two spheres—the Roman imperium at the beginning of the first century, Africa at the beginning of the twentieth—become especially apparent if one considers the theme, so important to Buchan, of imperial organization. At the time of Augustus' rise to power, Buchan repeatedly observes, the critical task for the Roman Empire had shifted from one of conquest and expansion to one of consolidation. The first emperor, having "no wish to increase the Roman territories" (Buchan, *Augustus*, 303), found himself charged with "the task of reshaping the empire," of "bring[ing] order out of chaos" (ibid., 69). Buchan's paradigmatic imperial hero (for clearly he considers him as such)[5] is thus not a conqueror but an administrator, giving shape and form to a culturally and ethnically diverse empire threatened with "disintegration," "anarchy," and chaos" (ibid., 331–33). With, then, the historical shift from a phase of imperial expansion to one of organization, Buchan imagines the concomitant emergence of an imperial hero especially well fitted to the latter work, figured as a form-bestowing subjectivity rather than a conquering warrior.

From Buchan's very first writings on the British Empire, which were based on his African experience, the former distinction is very much in evidence. In his early conversation novel, *A Lodge in the Wilderness* (1906), Buchan stages a series of quasi-Platonic dialogues on the theme of empire, set in the East African hideaway of a fictionalized Cecil Rhodes figure (Smith, *John Buchan*, 136). Late in the novel Lord Appin, former PM and formidably Hegelian dialectician,[6] distinguishes sharply between expansion and organization, reserving for the latter endeavor the true name of imperialism. Appin warns against any knee-jerk enthusiasm for mere "spacial [*sic*] extension" (ibid., 298) as a nostrum for national ills, noting that "Jingoism . . . is not a crude Imperialism; it is Imperialism's stark opposite" (ibid., 301). The real "aim" of "Imperialism, sanely considered," he concludes,

> is not conquest but consolidation and development, and its task within
> its own borders is so great that it has little inducement to meddle with its
> neighbours. . . . England has completed her great era of expansion. Her
> work for ages was to find new outlets for the vigour of her sons, and to
> occupy the waste or derelict places of the earth. Now, the land being won,
> it is her task to develop the wilds, to unite the scattered settlements, and
> to bring the whole within the influence of her tradition and faith. (ibid.,
> 301–2)

Underlying, of course, any discussion about the future of the British Empire in Buchan's time was the stark fact of its territorial arrest, the knowledge that a process of unprecedentedly rapid and extensive expansion had come to a sudden end. This sense of spatial exhaustion is well captured, in less sanguine tones than Appin's, by a would-be adventurer in the later *The Three Hostages,* who complains:

> Since the beginning of the century we've made a clean sweep of the jolly old mysteries that made the world worth living in. We have been to both the Poles, and to Lhasa, and to the Mountains of the Moon. . . . Mecca and Medina are as stale as Bournemouth. We know that there's nothing very stupendous in the Brahmaputra gorges. There's little left for a man's imagination to play with, and our children will grow up in a dull, shrunken world. (*The Three Hostages,* 242)

The language here belongs to the domain of geographic exploration—a pursuit itself by no means unentangled with the work of colonialism—but the sentiment exactly parallels the colonial situation by the early twentieth century, the reality that the great European powers essentially had nowhere else to go—no further cartographical space to color (in Britain's case) red. (Long superannuated was the map of white blanks that had given Conrad's Marlow such anticipatory delight.)

One critic invokes this historical reality as a possible explanation for Buchan's identification with the British imperial system, adducing a constitutional reverence for the powers that be (*whatever* they might, in fact, be), paired with a deeply felt aversion to the figure of the rebel: "Thus when a Buchan hero fought it was on the side of Zeus [rather than Prometheus]—of law and order and the established system—and by 1900 the British Empire was very much established, requiring maintenance and defense rather than extension" (Kruse, *John Buchan,* 23).

I want to argue here for another consequence of this fact of history for Buchan's thinking about empire: namely, that the perceived transition from a phase of imperial expansion to one of organization also involved a conceptual shift that tended to find expression in tropes of symbolic propagation, interpretation, and struggle. Beneath these tropes may be discerned a conception of information which fuses together its multiple senses, both residual and emergent: in Buchan's hands it is both symbolic material and an actively ordering, form-imposing force. In his classic study of adventure fiction from (roughly) Defoe to the First World War, Martin Green argues for the symbiotic relationship between that narrative tradition and empire, using a vocabulary of energy and movement which foregrounds, unsurprisingly given the historical parameters involved, the expansionist character of (particularly British) imperialism during this period. Such tales, he writes, constituted "the energizing myth of English imperialism . . . they charged England's will with the energy to go out into the world and explore, conquer, and rule" (Green, *Dreams of Adventure*, 3). But for Buchan, writing near the end of this phase of history, imperial energies were best devoted to projects of order: the imposition of form upon human fluxes swarming within delimited colonial spaces, often in rivalry with hostile systems or networks.

Such a paradigm, which would inform all of Buchan's thinking about empire, emerged fully grown in his early writing about Africa and the work of colonial reconstruction. In these texts one finds, instead of the old tropes of inscription (the conceit, for example, of filling in blanks on a map), a complex of related figures all connected with what one might call a master trope of *coding*. Here I find that Fredric Jameson's selective application of Deleuze and Guattari's thought to the modernist literary moment provides a useful conceptual framework for considering such a trope, or set of tropes. In his essay on "the ideology of modernism," Jameson extracts a historical metanarrative from the *Anti-Oedipus*, one premising a formless, "primordial flux that underlies experience itself"—the conceptual fiction to which Deleuze and Guattari give the name of schizophrenia—"which is then, in the various social forms, ordered into some more elaborate, but also clearly, in one way or another, more repressive structures . . . organized social life in one way or another then *codes* this initial flux . . . " (Jameson, "Beyond the Cave," 11). This basic model, with its core dynamic involving a kind of primal stuff, formless in itself but highly susceptible to formation, deformation, and reformation by exposure to *in*forming codes, is then used to underwrite a specific historical account from which can be derived a kind of taxonomy of moves or actions all springing from a common conceptual base (there is in Jameson's adaptation not only "coding" but "decoding," "recoding," even "overcoding"):

> the savage state is the moment of the coding of the original or primordial schizophrenic flux; in barbarism we have then to do with a more complex construction on this basis, which will be called an overcoding of it; under capitalism, reality undergoes a new type of operation or manipulation, and the desacralization or laicisation [*sic*], the quantification and rationalization of capitalism will be characterized by Deleuze and Guattari precisely as a decoding of these earlier types of realities or code-constructions; while finally, our own time . . . is marked by nothing quite so much as a recoding of this henceforth decoded flux—by *attempts* to recode, to reinvent the sacred, to go back to myth . . . in brief, that whole host of recoding strategies which characterize the various modernisms. . . . (ibid., 12–13)

Whatever its limitations as a factual account of historical "reality" (ibid., 12), such a narrative is a compelling way to characterize a predominant nexus of conceptual material available to writers of the modernist period: Buchan's high modernist contemporaries did, in fact, tend to think in ways congruent with the above account (I will return to this notion)—probably not accidentally considering the technological Zeitgeist of their (to say nothing of Deleuze's, Guattari's, and Jameson's) time.

Interestingly (and no more accidentally), a strikingly similar conceptual framework operates within Buchan's oeuvre as well (a set of texts which few would be inclined to include within any canon populated by Eliot, Joyce, Woolf, et al.). Yet while the putative existence of a cultural space (which I will treat as a pervasive conceptual fiction) composed of the fragments of hopelessly shattered code-systems, susceptible to subsequent reorganization, -assembly, or -coding, might be blamed (by representatives of the high modernist tradition) on the Great War, or (by Jameson, ventriloquizing Deleuze and Guattari) on capitalism, in Buchan's early writings about the colonial world it is blamed, very largely, on the imperial project itself. In *The African Colony: Studies in the Reconstruction* (1903), Buchan offers "the average Englishman" (*African Colony,* xiv) a panoramic portrait of South Africa in the wake of the Boer War. In reading this text one is struck by the persistent depiction of Britain's chief African colony as a crowded field of cultural fragments and ruins, not a blank but a modernist "waste land." South Africa is described as "a museum of the wrecks of conquerors and races" (ibid., 3–4), a congeries of cultural "wreckage" now reduced to a state of political "flux" (ibid., xviii). Appropriately in a work concerned with colonial reconstruction rather than expansion, *The African Colony* bristles with images of shattered disorder, heaps of "ruins" (ibid., 7), "fragments" (ibid., 8), "relics" (ibid., 17), "*débris*" (ibid., 18), and the like: a tableau of colonial chaos in need of patient organization, the superimposition from above of a set of ordering codes.

Buchan's treatment of "the subject races" (ibid., 284) is particularly eloquent in this regard. In his discussion of "the native question" (ibid.) (as distinct from issues primarily concerning the Boer population), a picture emerges of a people recently liberated from the cultural code-systems which had imposed a degree of order onto them, reducing them to an invertebrate mass of impressionable humanity. Buchan writes of a "process of disintegration" (ibid., 286) set in motion by the destabilizing "solvents of white civilisation" (ibid., 297), solvents powerfully corrosive to pre-existing systems of "tribal customs and beliefs" (ibid., 287). Without this symbolic armature, the native population rapidly deliquesces into a formless mass, to be reckoned not in discrete units but as disconcertingly shapeless "efflux[es]" (ibid., 288) and "fluctuations" (ibid., 304). And with this "crumbling" of "the old tribal system" (ibid., 295), the "loosening" of "the old ties," comes a new threat to imperial order, since "in the mass [the native] forms an unknown quantity, compared with which a Paris mob is a Quaker meeting" (ibid., 290). "The wholly detribalised native" (ibid., 305), Buchan warns, is "a derelict creature without faith or stamina, having lost his old taboos, and being as yet unable to understand the laws of the white man" (ibid., 286). On the whole, however, in *The African Colony* Buchan appeals more to feelings of paternalistic benevolence than to fears of what dangers the "unknown quantity" of a "detribalised" population might present to imperial security. In arguing, for instance, for the need to bring the "formative" as well as the "solvent" "influences of civilisation" (ibid., 291) to bear upon the native population, Buchan observes that, "Since we are destroying the old life, with its moral and social codes . . . we are bound to provide an honest substitute" (ibid., 308).

However, he would give free rein to precisely such anxieties in the novel *Prester John* (1910), a work fed by fears that, in the absence of such reconstructive work, the deracinated native masses might be vulnerable to recoding by an imperial rival. Buchan's sixth novel is an adventure story whose protagonist, the young Scot David Crawfurd, is driven by the need to earn a living to a humble mercantile position in "Blaauw—something or other . . . in the far north of the Transvaal" (Buchan, *Prester John*, 20). There he finds himself enlisted in a desperate struggle to foil the schemes of John Laputa, the "great black minister" (ibid., 70) who would make himself a "[king] of Africa" (ibid., 202) by fomenting a native rebellion; he plans a massive, coordinated "rising, with diamonds as the sinews of war" (ibid., 69).[7] Laputa's plan to resurrect the ancient glory of Prester John's fabled domains by bringing into being the "Kaffir empire" envisioned by Shaka Zulu (ibid., 72) revolves around his possession of a mighty "fetich" (ibid.), the "necklet of Prester John" (ibid., 75). Claiming to be the ancient emperor's "incarnated spirit," returned "to lead the African race to conquest and empire" (ibid.), Laputa seeks to weld together the diverse mass of the native population ("Such a collection of races has never been seen" [ibid., 106]) into a frighteningly disciplined unity.

While my discernment of a master trope of coding in *The African Colony* may admittedly benefit from a sympathetic reading (in the earlier text Buchan does indeed speak of disarrayed "systems" of cultural "codes," but other conceptual metaphors might also be argued for), in *Prester John* the connection between technologies of coding and the prospect of organized native resistance is both explicit and pervasive. The novel is permeated with the figure of the information system—or rather, of warring information systems occupying the same space. In addition to their uncanny network of unseen drummers, whose signaling is so unsettling to the white man ("I have never heard an eerier sound," admits Crawfurd) (ibid., 62), Buchan's natives (like so many others') possess telepathic powers as well (why then do they need the drums?), while the Britons must rely on their insecure, embattled communications systems. The rivalry between systems is explicit, and articulated in terms familiar since the Indian Mutiny at least: "They are cunning fellows," warns the schoolmaster Wardlaw, "and have arts that we know nothing about. You have heard of native telepathy. They can send news over a thousand miles as quick as the telegraph, and we have no means of tapping the wires" (ibid., 54). It is, however, rather astonishing how Buchan's colonials elide any essential distinction between natural and supernatural networks here, treating both as technologies *tout court* and reckoning the powers of each in the most pragmatic terms: "We can't match their telepathy," Arcoll muses, "but the new type of field telegraph is not so bad, and may be a trifle more reliable" (ibid., 78). Hermann Wittenberg rightly aligns this telepathic system with "an intangible, indigenous semiotic order" ("Occult, Empire and Landscape," n.p.); along with the network of drum-signals, it is suggestive of dormant native code-systems, which might at any time be awakened if alternatives are not provided.

The dangers of recoding by a rival power are dramatized, again, in Laputa's plot to organize the native masses through his possession of Solomon's necklace—an instrument that should also be read as a "semiotic" or symbolic weapon, precursor to the many figurations of propaganda he would include in his later fiction. Buchan's early education, I believe, contributed to his creation of this conceit. During the painful upheavals—personal and societal—brought about by the Great War, Buchan, an accomplished classicist since youth, would find solace in returning to those "Latin and Greek classics which were beyond the caprice of time," in particular Plato, "for he was seraphically free from the pettinesses which were at the root of our sorrows" (*Pilgrim's Way*, 166). His singling out of Plato as an anodyne for an age of social and cultural convulsion is significant, as—I would argue—an essentially Platonic vision consistently underlies Buchan's thought. And, of course, alongside a supposedly "seraphic" indifference to the paltry, time-bound concerns of the sublunary world, any Platonist also inherits a particular "information theory," one rooted in a dualist vision, with a belief in both the primacy of ideas and their contingent embodiment in matter: as Jeremy Campbell writes in his *Grammatical Man: Information, Entropy, Language, and Life*, "Plato, too [as well as Aristotle], had an 'information' theory of a kind" (267). Similarly, Hans Christian von Baeyer begins his genealogical investigation of the concept of information (whose roots lie, again, in the idea of a shaping force) with Plato: "The word 'form' entered Western philosophy as a translation of Plato's word *eidos*, the root of the words 'idea' and 'ideal'" (*Information*, 20).[8]

Long before Buchan was put in charge of British of propaganda, before, indeed, he arrived in Africa as an agent of colonial reconstruction, he was thus, I would suggest, powerfully inclined to think in terms of a transcendent *eidos* of Empire acting upon receptive matter. This helps to explain, no doubt, how Buchan came to develop the conceit of the symbolic or ideational weapon, of which Prester John's necklace is only the first incarnation in his fiction. Laputa's secret weapon is (no less than any propagandistic text) literally a string or chain of symbols: "There were fifty-five rubies in it, the largest as big as a pigeon's egg, and the least not smaller than my thumbnail. In shape they were oval, cut on both sides *en cabochon*, and on each certain characters were engraved" (*Prester John*, 103). This potent "fetich" is symbolic, too, in a further sense: being an embodiment of Idea stamped upon matter, it is itself powerfully emblematic of Laputa's top-down imposition of order upon his native followers. It is also the first of a series of symbolic weapons Buchan imagined as posing a grave threat to British imperial stability.

With *Prester John*, then, Buchan had discovered both a favorite MacGuffin[9] and a kind of master narrative template for it to occupy. During the following decade, and particularly with the advent of the Great War, Britain's imperial anxieties would shift ground significantly, while at the same time Buchan's understanding of the "informing" techniques and technologies available to modern societies was continually expanded, modified and refined. By examining the series of novels which appeared during these years, in which Buchan rehearsed variants of his master scenario within these changing contexts, I will trace both that evolving conception and its enduringly central importance to the novelist's thinking about empire. It is to these novels that I now turn.

III.

Richard Hannay, the protagonist of *Greenmantle* (1916),[10] goes undercover as a virulently anti-British Boer in hopes of discovering the secret "card" (Buchan, *Greenmantle*, 13) which Germany intends to play in order to unite the Muslim world against the British Empire. He tries what one might call a homeopathic tactic, outlining for the fearsome officer Colonel von Stumm a similar project, ostensibly of his own devising, in an attempt to draw the real German plan out of him. Interestingly, Hannay's proposition is essentially, and more or less avowedly, cribbed from *Prester John*: it is as if the hero of Buchan's Great War novels were a fan of his earlier work. Urging Stumm to concentrate on the African theater of war[11] ("England will not let East Africa go. She fears for Egypt and she fears, too, for India. . . . She cares more for her Empire than for what may happen to her allies") (ibid., 53), Hannay argues for the need to unify the native "mass" (ibid.) through some ideological tool or weapon. In so doing he invokes not only Laputa's (fictional) scheme but also the memory of other, historically real threats to Britain's African empire (the Zulu, the Mahdi):

> You need men, and the men are waiting. They are black, but they are the stuff of warriors. All round your borders you have the remains of great fighting tribes, the Angoni, the Masai, the Manyumwezi, and above all the Somalis of the north, and the dwellers on the upper Nile. The British recruit their black regiments there, and so do you. But to get recruits is not enough. You must set whole nations moving, as the Zulu under Tchaka flowed over South Africa. . . .
>
> The black man obeys [the European] and puts away his gods, but he worships them all the time in his soul. We must get his gods on our side, and then he will move mountains. We must do as John Laputa did with Sheba's necklace. . . .
>
> First find the race that fears its priests. It is waiting for you—the Mussulmans of Somaliland and the Abyssinian border and the Blue and White Nile. They would be like dried grasses to catch fire if you used the flint and steel of their religion. Look what the English suffered from a crazy Mullah who ruled only a dozen villages. Once get the flames going and they will lick up the pagans of the west and south. That is the way of Africa. How many thousands, think you, were in the Mahdi's army who never heard of the Prophet till they saw the black flags of the Emirs going into battle? (ibid., 54)

As Hannay's reference here to the plot of *Prester John* suggests,[12] by now Buchan has established something like a stock narrative formula, to be found not only at the heart of both of these novels but also in texts like *Mr Standfast* and *The Three Hostages* as well. In *Greenmantle*, that is, just as in the earlier novel of colonial adventure, the central (and here eponymous) MacGuffin is an ideational or conceptual weapon. Indeed, while Buchan's World War I novels invoke the specters of both chemical and biological warfare,[13] far and away the most ominous threat faced by the British Empire in the Hannay novels is, once more, that of *symbolic* warfare, in the form of a sign or talisman which would "inform" an essentially shapeless people, welding its potentially dangerous but inchoate mass into a focused unity.

This time around, it is imperial Germany—Britain's imperial doppelganger—in possession of the information weapon, and the ultimate stakes for Britain are nothing less than "the de-molition," as the American Blenkiron quaintly puts it in another context, "of the British Empire" (ibid., 29). Germany's territorial ambitions (expressed by such familiar tropes as a map on which, as Stumm arrogantly prophesies, the British red will be replaced by the German yellow) center first and foremost upon the Near East: "Germany," one of its officers opines, "could gobble up the French and the Russians whenever she cared, but she was aiming at getting all the Middle East in her hands first, so that she could come out conqueror with the practical control of half the world" (ibid., 45–46). To this end the Germans mean to fuse the Islamic world into a cohesive war machine, recognizing, as Hannay puts it, that "religion is the only thing to knit up such a scattered empire" (ibid., 12). "Greenmantle," their secret weapon, is to the Muslim mind "[a] seer . . . of the blood of the Prophet, who will restore the Khalifate to its old glories and Islam to its old purity" (ibid., 147). While ostensibly a matter of "blood," however, the purely symbolic nature of the position is revealed by its ready capacity for sartorial construction[14]: when the "real" Greenmantle dies, Sandy, dressed up in "emerald coat and turban" (ibid., 271), himself becomes Greenmantle; in the novel's dramatic conclusion it is this "Greenmantle," a "dark sheen of emerald" (ibid., 272) on horseback, who leads a mounted host to victory *against* the pro-German forces.

But if Buchan's Great War novels are to a large extent founded on a kind of recycled ur-plot based upon an information weapon, they also represent an ongoing process of conceptual evolution, in which Buchan continues to explore and refine the idea of information. To a large extent, these novels of imperial conflict serve, indeed, as allegories for the emergence of the modern information society, particularly its debts to the context of an imperialist war. Throughout the Hannay novels (particularly strikingly, as I will show, in the cases of Ivery in *Mr Standfast* and Medina in *The Three Hostages*), Buchan's villains seem positively to invite the reader to interpret them in light of their relationship to particular conceptions of information. *Greenmantle* is no exception. In the novel, the German imperial threat is distributed between two figures: the bullet-headed man-mountain Stumm ("the German of caricature . . . hideous as a hippopotamus, but effective" [ibid., 50]) and the even more dangerous Frau Hilda von Einem ("The woman frightens me into fits," admits Hannay [ibid., 187]). There are, of course, numerous respects in which these two greatly dissimilar adversaries of the British Empire, the hulking bully and the bewitching femme fatale, constitute a study in contrasts. But in the present context, I want to focus on the strikingly opposed conceptions of information and its uses which the two figures hold, indeed seem to embody.

As his name signals, Stumm (German for "silent" or "dumb") is associated throughout the novel with a policy of total information blackout. Secrets must be kept secure at all costs; their keepers must (as the contemporary British slang phrase puts it) "keep schtum."[15] The colonel would wholeheartedly have agreed with the slogan coined during the next world war, *Loose lips sink ships,* and would probably have shuddered with distaste if he had heard Blenkiron's use of a Carnotian metaphor blithely equating the circulation of information with a fissiparous thermodynamic system: "Officially we [Americans] do nothing except give off Notes like a leaky boiler gives off steam" (ibid., 21).[16] Virtually every episode in which Stumm appears contains some evidence of his passion for secrecy and information control, his terror of leakage. Examples include his first, suspicious denial to Hannay and Pienaar of the very existence of the Greenmantle project ("We have no secret," he insists irritably [ibid., 55]), his annoyed response to the garrulous Blenkiron's attempts at conversation on sensitive subjects ("Stumm pointed to a notice which warned officers to refrain from discussing military operations with mixed company in a railway carriage" [ibid., 62]), and his attempts to seal off Germany's borders to prevent the escape of the intelligence agent Hannay, who has obtained valuable "information" (ibid., 100). It is a fitting irony that in the end his nemesis not only escapes from his supposedly escape-proof prison, an ostensibly closed system like the impenetrable kraal of the parable ("You will be safer with me than in the town gaol," he purrs in premature triumph, "for it's a trifle draughty. It lets things in, and it might let things out" [ibid., 208]), but manages the theft of critical information from Stumm's "private cabinet" in the process.

Von Einem, on the other hand, represents a radically different, indeed antithetical, conception of information's strategic value to the Fatherland. Where Stumm wishes to keep information locked up, her own master plan centers precisely upon symbolic production and circulation. Again, of the novel's two villains, this "female devil" (ibid., 162) is clearly the more dangerous (even her allies fear her), and this fact is surely related to her status as the text's master-propagandist, a figure devoted (as the etymology of the word suggests) to a war of symbolic propagation rather than concealment. Appropriately enough, Hannay—and the reader—first encounter von Einem in conspicuously symbolic form, as a coded segment of a riddling sequence scrawled by a dying British agent, and introduced in the first chapter ("on [the paper] were written three words—'*Kasredin*,' '*cancer*,' and '*v.I.*'" [ibid., 15]). Later in the novel Hannay, recovering from a bout of fever, stumbles upon the secret of the third word:

> *v.I*—that was the worst gibberish of all.
>
> Before this I had always taken the *I* as the letter of the alphabet. I had thought that the *v.* must stand for *von*, and had considered the German names beginning with I. . . . Now I found myself taking the *I* as the numeral One. Idly, not thinking what I was doing, I put it into German.
>
> Then I nearly fell out of bed. *Von Einem* . . . (ibid., 98)

To a twenty-first-century reader, this derivation (Einem from "One") is highly suggestive. Between them, these two agents of an expansionist German Empire might be said to stand for the primal ingredients of information itself, as it would come to be formulated as a binary entity: Stumm, the principle of silence or absence, stands for the *zero;* Einem (or I), the principle of symbolic presence and proliferation, is of course the *one.*

But if in *Greenmantle* Buchan relies heavily on emergent conceptualizations of information in figuring the representatives of Britain's hated counter-empire, he at the same time celebrates information as something like a quasi-religious principle or symbol of order and human communion. Of course, his heroes as well as his villains are information warriors. They embody, indeed, a kind of distributed system of heroism, whose components are pointedly aligned with distinctive tactics of coding and simulation (Blenkiron, incapable of first-order dissimulation, is the master of the "double bluff," Sandy Arbuthnot the Burtonian master of tongues and disguises, and so on). They prevail in the end quite simply because they *win* the information war, stealing Stumm's plan of the Erzerum defenses and transferring it to the Russians ("by hook or by crook, we've got to get that information through to them" [ibid., 226]), and simultaneously scuttling von Einem's propaganda campaign ("We've got to blow the whole Greenmantle business so high that the bits of it will never come to earth again" [ibid.]).

But there is a remarkable scene, late in the novel, in which Buchan goes much further than this, figuring information as a kind of transcendental agent of meaning in a world in danger of becoming meaningless. In the late chapter, "Peter Pienaar Goes to the Wars," the faithful Boer is sent with Stumm's plans to the front lines, to practice his preternatural powers of "veld-craft," learned in colonial Africa ("he had a kind of 'feel' for the landscape, a special sense which is born in savages and can only be acquired after long experience by the white man" [ibid., 233]). Pienaar has to get past the trenches unseen, all the while avoiding being blown to bits by artillery. The Anatolian front is the Eastern counterpart to the blood-soaked fields of Belgium and France, and Buchan does not shrink from depicting the horrors of this sort of war: "He [Pienaar] told me [Hannay] it was exactly what the predikant used to say that Hell would be like" (ibid., 235), a nightmare land lit by "calcium rockets and Verey flares" (ibid.) and saturated with heavy artillery.

More, Buchan depicts the battlefield in a fashion that is consistent with its treatment in such key documents of high modernism as "The Waste Land," namely as a shattered space of fragments and ruins, in which chaos and unmeaning "noise" reign—what might be termed the modernist Great War chronotope:

> Peter felt very sick. He had not believed there could be so much noise in the world, and the drums of his ears were splitting. . . . Peter lay on the crest, watching the shells burst, and confident that any moment he might be a shattered remnant. (ibid.)

But if this episode contains Buchan's version of a familiar modernist narrative of devastation and fragmentation, it also points to his own distinctive vision of recoding, one imaginatively derived from information systems. As Pienaar, "brought . . . to his senses" by falling onto a corpse in a trench ("That men could die at all seemed a comforting, homely thing after that unnatural pandemonium" [ibid., 236]), continues to crawl through the fragmented space of the battlefield, past "the debris of walls" and the "ruins" of buildings (ibid.), he comes across a Turkish communication trench, "which ran through [a] ruined building" (ibid., 237). The meaningless din of battle having been succeeded by an empty silence, Pienaar now discerns the presence of meaning, in the form of a zero-degree signal, broadcast over the waste land:

> Suddenly a curious sound fell on his ears. It was so faint that at first he doubted the evidence of his senses. Then as the wind fell it came louder. It was exactly like some hollow piece of metal being struck by a stick, musical and oddly resonant.
>
> He concluded it was the wind blowing a branch of a tree against an old boiler in the ruin before him. . . .
>
> But as he listened he caught the note again. It was a bell, a fallen bell, and the place before him must have been a chapel. He remembered that an Armenian monastery had been marked on the big map, and he guessed it was the burned building on his right.

The thought of a chapel and a bell gave him the notion of some human agency. And then suddenly the notion was confirmed. The sound was regular and concerted—dot, dash, dot—dash, dot, dot. The branch of a tree and the wind may play strange pranks, but they do not produce the longs and shorts of the Morse Code.

This was where Peter's intelligence work in the Boer War helped him. He knew the Morse, he could read it, but he could make nothing of the signalling. It was either in some special code or in a strange language. (ibid., 237–38)

The signaler proves to be an ally: an anti-Enver Turk working with the Russians. He has improvised, in true *bricoleur* fashion, an aural field-telegraph, and is in communication with the Russians. Pienaar convinces him to send a message warning of his (Pienaar's) arrival with valuable information, and once again the silent, scarred battlefield echoes with the sound of human communication:

The man took the blunt end of his bayonet and squatted beside the bell. The first stroke brought out a clear, searching note which floated down the valley. He struck three notes at slow intervals. For all the world, Peter said, he was like a telegraph operator calling up a station. . . .

After ten minutes the man ceased and listened. From far away came the sound of a trench-gong, the kind of thing they used on the Western Front to give the gas-alarm. (ibid, 241)

Particularly when taken in the context of Buchan's larger treatment of information, this episode strikes me too as "oddly resonant" (Pienaar's phrase for the sound of the bayonet-struck church bell). As I hint above, it is, I think, instructive to read such scenes as this one alongside the range of high modernist responses to the horrors of modern war, understood as agent of cultural devastation and fragmentation. In the now-classic reading, figures like Eliot, Joyce, and others should be understood as engaging in a variety of artistic strategies—the imposition of myth, the shoring of fragments against ruins—in an attempt to map some sort of order onto the chaos of modernity; Jameson writes, again, of "that whole host of recoding strategies which characterize the various modernisms" (Jameson, "Beyond the Cave," 13). The above episode, I would suggest, should be read as a compression of Buchan's own, overarching "recoding strategy," one in which information itself, increasingly charged with symbolic resonance, comes to stand for such an ordering principle.

In the numb silence succeeding the unmeaning cacophony of war, Buchan imagines the emergence of pure signal, information in a kind of pristine form, recoding a space of fragments and ruins. (The improvised field-telegraph's use of bells, recalling the technology's origins,[17] adds perhaps a note of renascence or rebirth here.) For Shannon, "information" would become something rigorously distinct from "meaning." But for Buchan, as the poetic tableau of plangent bell-strokes of Morse code "[floating] down the valley" suggests, there was something profoundly meaningful about information, even distinct from semantic content (the first exchange is purely phatic to Pienaar). Nor, surely, is the conspicuous presence of the religious element (the church-bell, the wrecked monastery) accidental here. More and more, Buchan is coming to view information itself as the privileged binding agent for a modern world in which older code-systems lie in ruins.

In an essay on "The Villain in the Spy Novels of John Buchan," Philip E. Ray proposes to trace "the historical significance of the typical Buchan villain" (Ray, "Villain," 82), convincingly arguing that one of Buchan's great imaginative achievements was to blend the stock German agent of a Le Queux or Childers novel with elements of the fanatical Conradian or Chestertonian anarchist (though curiously enough the essay does not consider either *Greenmantle* or *Mr Standfast*). As my above reading of the figures of Stumm and Hilda von Einem would indicate, however, I believe that any attempt to read historically "the Buchan villain" must also take into account his ongoing engagement with the emergent conceptualization of information in the modern world—particularly as these figures so frequently serve as screens onto which the novelist projects its frightening potentialities. Read in this light, Moxon Ivery, the central adversary of *Mr Standfast* (Buchan's next Great War thriller and third Hannay novel), represents the next stage in this recurrent type's imaginative evolution.

Ivery, a holdover from *The Thirty-Nine Steps* (he was a member of the "Black Stone" gang), is really the "Graf von Schwabing," a German agent described in the novel as "the most dangerous man in all the world" (Buchan, *Mr Standfast*, 22). Hiding in plain sight as an English gentleman of pacifist convictions,[18] Ivery is really the proverbial "spider" (ibid., 43) at the center of a vast, uncannily potent German information system. Fascinatingly, he himself *embodies* such a system as well: he is a "chameleon" (ibid., 159), a shape-shifter with astonishing powers of self-transformation yet, disconcertingly, few if any stable marks of identity to call his own. When Hannay first encounters Ivery, the only distinctive feature he discerns is, appropriately enough, his voice: "he was the genuine silver-tongue" (ibid., 33); visually he is figured as a virtual blank slate, an utter absence of both form and hue:

a plump middle-aged man, with a colourless face and nondescript features. . . . I watched him, fascinated, studying his face carefully; and the thing that struck me was that there was nothing in it—nothing, that is to say, to lay hold on. . . . I noticed that there were hardly any lines on [his face]. . . . He had a pleasant smile which made his jaw and cheeks expand like India-rubber. (ibid., 33–35)

Indeed, Blenkiron seems hardly to be speaking metaphorically when he says of Ivery's countenance, "It isn't a face, it's a mask. He could make himself look like Shakespeare or Julius Caesar or Billy Sunday or Brigadier-General Richard Hannay if he wanted to" (ibid., 46). At one point, the terror of an air raid causes Ivery's concentration to slip, and he lapses into a more radical formlessness, a "transformation" witnessed by an astonished Hannay (in a scene which, surely, could be creditably rendered on screen only in our own age of CGI technology):

Then I gasped with amazement, for I saw that it was Ivery.
And yet it was not Ivery. There were the familiar nondescript features, the blandness, the plumpness, but all, so to speak, in ruins. The man was in a blind funk. His features seemed to be dislimning before my eyes. He was growing sharper, finer, in a way younger, a man without grip on himself, a shapeless creature in process of transformation. He was being reduced to his rudiments. (ibid., 146)

The German master of information, supremely adept at channeling intelligence and circulating propaganda, is himself without essential form, though able to shape his flesh into infinite forms. He thus himself epitomizes or literalizes a supremely efficient information system: he has only to concentrate, and ideational forms are embodied, with infinite ease and swiftness.

But Ivery also represents another prospect profoundly disturbing to Buchan: the idea of an enemy without any set of stable values or codes underlying the play of simulation. In this regard Ivery is not merely Hannay's nemesis but also his foil. There are, indeed, a number of respects in which Ivery functions as a kind of double for Hannay, even taking on the role, uncharacteristically enough in the series, of sexual rival. Most obviously, perhaps, both are masters of disguise, capable of adopting a seemingly infinite number of forms. But beneath the succession of shifting surfaces, the reader perceives in Hannay a bedrock of British virtues: he is undeniably a gentleman, a Christian, and the very soul of honor, abundantly possessed of the classic public-school values ("fair play," and so on). Hannay, in short, conjures with form in the ultimate service of an underlying code or set of codes. Ivery, on the other hand, is utterly devoid of "honour," as the reader is more than once reminded.[19] Indeed, despite his aristocratic title, the Graf von Schwabing is not a "gentleman" at all, as Buchan takes curiously elaborate pains to establish, as in the speech he puts in the mouth of Blenkiron:

> Your German aristocracy can't consort on terms of equality with any other Upper Ten. They swagger and bluff about the world, but they know very well that the world's sniggering at them. They're like a boss from Salt Creek Gully who's made his pile and bought a dress suit and dropped into a Newport evening party. They don't know where to put their hands or how to keep their feet still. . . . Your copper-bottomed English nobleman has got to keep jogging himself to treat them as equals instead of sending them down to the servants' hall. . . . That's why when a Graf is booted out of the Fatherland, he's got to creep back somehow or be a wandering Jew for the rest of time. (ibid., 206–7)

For the German—*any* German, according to Blenkiron ("They're a pecooliar people, a darned pecooliar people," he muses [ibid., 206]), aristocracy is merely another, if uniquely challenging, performance, one impossible to pull off away from his native soil.[20] When Ivery is finally defeated, Hannay (in what might be termed a meta-gloat) says, "when I was in your power, you indulged your vanity by gloating over me. I expected it, for your class does not breed gentlemen" (ibid., 282). Then a bit later, just in case the reader may have missed the point, Buchan cannot resist inserting the following exchange between the two adversaries:

> "Why do you degrade me? I am a gentleman."
> "Not as we define the thing," I said. (ibid., 300)

Without morals, regard for law, a code of honor, or even a stable class identity—all are simply further disguises for him, precise counterparts to the contingent forms he impresses upon the blank of his face—Ivery-Schwabing is at bottom an uncoded cipher. He is thus a nightmare figure conceptually indebted to information itself, particularly when it is wielded without scruple.

Similarly nightmarish is the information system to which Ivery stands, again, in both a metaphoric and a metonymic relation. Indeed, perhaps the greatest anxiety underlying the novel is the specter of the secret network. Ivery is repeatedly figured as a spider in the center of a vast web, one whose strands stretch from Russia to the American West to the secret "post office"

(44) Hannay discovers in the Scottish Highlands. Later in the novel, the figure of the secret network finds its consummation in Ivery's vaunted "Underground Railway," essentially a gothicized information system:

> You have heard of the Untergrundbahn? No? And you boast of an Intelligence service! Yet your ignorance is shared by the whole of your General Staff. It is a little organization of my own. By it we can take unwilling and dangerous people inside our frontier to be dealt with as we please. Some have gone from England and many from France. Officially I believe they are recorded as "missing," but they did not go astray on any battlefield. . . . (ibid., 241)

That the network is the (distributed, circulatory) equivalent to the immobile Radcliffean castle or abbey is shown by Ivery's plan to make Hannay's beloved Mary disappear into it ("[W]e shall be a merry party in the Underground Express," he says tauntingly [ibid.]). Indeed, the very mention of the "Untergrundbahn" invariably awakes a degree of terror in Buchan's heroes which might seem disproportionate ("'The Underground Railway!' [Wake] groaned. 'The thought of it drives me mad'" [ibid., 253]),[21] unless it be the case that the deepest anxiety is generated here by the very idea of the secret network itself.

As Thomas Richards observes, the years following the Franco-Prussian War saw the emergence in Britain of a paranoid fantasy of "an enemy archive," "a parallel but alien construction of comprehensive knowledge" (Thomas, *Imperial Archive*, 113). While the fantasy of the archive of the imperial other was to some extent a detachable one, for clear historical reasons it was most often attached to Germany during this period (ibid., 111–13). Yet the trope of the secret network differs significantly from that of the counter-archive coterminous with the territory of the rival nation-state. In novels like *Mr Standfast*, Europe becomes a palimpsest of multiple, overlapping networks, with the real war taking place precisely at the level of contending information systems occupying the same territory: Ivery's sprawling "web"; the official network of telegraph, post, and telephone that serves British state power; and the vast secret network administered, as the reader learns, by Blenkiron—a system which he sees as necessary supplement to the British Intelligence Service he "reverence[s]" (*Mr Standfast*, 43).[22] Wartime Europe is thus depicted as thoroughly overcoded; much as Buchan had seen the project of "reconstruction" in southern Africa in terms of the succession of tropes of expansion by those of coding, his depiction of the domestic struggle of imperial powers is figured as a kind of implosion. There are thus good historical reasons, linked with the modern history of imperialism, for the emergence of the spy thriller or, as it might be termed, novel of information war, at just this time. At the moment when the great imperial powers found themselves engaged in murderous battles for infinitesimal patches of ground, its imagined information warriors (in contradistinction to the adventurer-heroes of an age of expansion) cohabit a sharply circumscribed field shot through with warring code-systems. It is surely not without significance that this early example of the genre has its own code-book or key text, to which many of its own characters, events, and chapters (as well as, of course, its title) correspond: Bunyan's *Pilgrim's Progress,* itself an exemplary embodiment of the "overcoded" narrative mode of allegory, a mode premised upon the dense coexistence of multiple levels of meaning within the same textual "space."

IV.

In *The Three Hostages,* Buchan gives Hannay (now ensconced in comfortable retirement in the Cotswolds) a new nemesis, Dominick Medina, in whom one may discern the apotheosis of the novelist's vision of information as ultimate weapon, particularly in the hands of an imperial or colonial other. Medina, "a propagandist of genius" (Buchan, *Three Hostages,* 133, 255), is an irresistibly attractive figure of irreproachable character, with a brilliant political future ahead of him (publicly he intends to ride the wave of a "mighty Tory revival" (ibid., 54) all the way, perhaps, to Downing Street). In reality, however, his ambitions are far greater, and more destructive. Like Ivery, Medina is secretly (though to the alert reader not particularly surprisingly) the "master mind" (ibid., 49) of a vast, invisible network, a criminal gang making use of the masses of anarchists and other "moral imbeciles" produced by the war: "The moral imbecile . . . had been more or less a sport before the War; now he was a terribly common product, and throve in batches and battalions" (ibid., 23). Again the reader encounters the by now familiar Buchan trope of an inchoate mass informed by diabolical forces ("there were sinister brains at work to organize for their own purposes the perilous stuff lying about" [ibid., 24]), and once more the prime mover of the plot is an archetypal figure fashioned from contemporary conceptions of the nature, and potential dangers, of information. While Ivery was a Proteus, able to impress ideas directly upon the medium of his own flesh, Medina, a master hypnotist, represents the terrifying prospect of techniques of thought control so potent that they work without the participation of any medium at all. He wields the power of direct, unmediated "spirit on spirit" (64), using it first to reprogram the "three hostages" of the title, snatched by his gang as an insurance policy, and then to transform (he believes) Hannay into his personal slave.

The novel, indeed, written in the aftermath of Buchan's multifaceted work as propagandist in the war, contains his most explicit treatment of propaganda as a form of mind control: at one symposium of elites at a London club it is asserted that "the great offensives of the future [will] be psychological" (ibid., 64), and "that the most deadly weapon in the world [is] the power of mass-persuasion" (ibid., 64–65). Medina, able to wipe clean the slate of the mind and reinscribe it as he likes (except in the case of Hannay, constitutionally "unsympathetic" [ibid., 71] and thus immune to such mental meddling), is thus in one sense simply the latest incarnation of the propagandist figures of Buchan's earlier thrillers: Laputa, von Einem, Ivery. However, there are impor-tant differences in *The Three Hostages,* differences reflecting both new devel-opments and new anxieties associated with this moment in British imperial history: crucially, in this novel information warfare is also waged against Brit-ish elites (the above-mentioned manipulation of masses of "moral imbeciles" pales, indeed, in comparison to this new threat), and it is waged by a figure representing not an imperial rival but a conflation of Britain's own (present and former) colonial population.[23]

These two differences are in fact closely related, and together they reflect the historical context in which the novel was written. The period after the First World War generated widespread anxiety in Britain about both social and cultural disintegration in general and imperial disintegration in par-ticular; the historian Lawrence James, mentioning Buchan as one popular representative of this pessimistic Zeitgeist,[24] writes of a general belief in a "protean force which appeared not only unstoppable, but threatened the exis-tence of the empire" (James, *Rise and Fall,* 371). The fear of imperial dissolu-tion seemed to find confirmation in a series of recent events in the colonial world, of which the most conspicuous were the withdrawal of Ireland from the imperial system and the mass riots, prompted by Gandhi's anti-imperial activities, which generated fears of "a second mutiny" in India (ibid., 372).

Buchan's depiction of Medina draws upon both of these theaters of impe-rial dissolution—consummated and dreaded—in order to exploit the anxieties they engendered back home. First of all, and despite his seemingly flawless patina of Englishness, Medina in fact comes from an old Irish family, one whose ancestral antagonism towards England is embodied without disguise in his blind mother, a terrifying figure who lurks like Lady Macbeth (Buchan, *Three Hostages,* 139) behind the scenes, urging him on to ever greater atroci-ties. Animated by pure hatred, she represents a demonized version (from an Anglocentric perspective) of the Gaelic matriarch:

She sat in the high-backed chair . . . as if it were a throne. The firelight lit her face, and I saw that it was very old, waxen with age. . . . Her dress was straight and black like a gaberdine, and she had thick folds of lace at her wrists and neck. Wonderful hair, masses of it, was piled on her head, and it was snow-white and fine as silk. . . . Blind though [her eyes] were, they seemed to radiate an ardent vitality, to glow and flash like the soul within.

I realized that it was the most wonderful face of a woman I had ever looked on. And I realized in the same moment that I hated it, that the beauty of it was devilish, and the soul within was on fire with all the hatred of Hell . . . they [Medina and his mother] spoke for the most part in a language of which I did not know a word—it may have been Choctaw, but was probably Erse. . . . This woman was the Blind Spinner of the rhymes. No doubt of it. I could see her spinning beside a peat fire, nursing ancient hate and madness, and crooning forgotten poetry. (ibid., 107–12)

The smell of burning peat in fact accompanies mother Medina throughout the novel as a kind of olfactory stain, one of the ineradicable signifiers of a primeval, and hostile, Irishness attached to her (in one episode Hannay, blindfolded, reports: "There was a scent in the air which anywhere else I would have sworn was due to peat smoke, and mixed with it another intangible savour which I could not put a name to, but which did not seem to belong to London at all, or to any dwelling, but to some wild out-of-doors" [ibid., 83–84]; later, entering Medina's study, he observes, ominously, "I smelt more than wood smoke; there was peat burning among the oak billets" [ibid., 107]).

Significantly, Buchan deliberately selects what are (for him at least) emotionally polyvalent signs of Irishness, sensory cues capable of multiple associations: Hannay also mentions "the hundred times when I had sniffed peat-reek in happy places" (ibid.). This is because Buchan wants to depict not only a sinister Ireland *per se*, but also, and more particularly, the dark side of what he sees as contemporaneous Irish propaganda, the deployment of an armament of homely, rustic symbols in the service of a plot to cast a spell over the British public, and especially its decision makers. It is no accident that, in the novel's (and one of the novelist's) most explicit discussions of propaganda work, Buchan's prime example is not "that damned German propaganda" (*Greenmantle*, 183) but Ireland's campaign (as he sees it) of virtual mind control against the English. The detective Macgillivray, in describing to Hannay how Scotland Yard has been able to "put a spoke in the wheels of some of [the gang's] worst enterprises" (*Three Hostages,* 49) unwittingly (no one suspects Medina as yet) directs the reader's attention to the land of his ancestry:

Also we have put a brake on their propaganda side. They are masters of propaganda, you know. Dick, have you ever considered what a diabolical weapon that can be—using all the channels of modern publicity to poison and warp men's minds? It is the most dangerous thing on earth. You can use it cleanly—as I think on the whole we did in the War—but you can also use it to establish the most damnable lies. . . . Look at the Irish! They are the cleverest propagandists extant, and managed to persuade most people that they were a brave, generous, humorous, talented, warmhearted race, cruelly yoked to a dull mercantile England, when God knows they were exactly the opposite. (ibid., 50)

Hannay mentions in an aside to the reader that "Macgillivray . . . is an Ulsterman, and has his prejudices" (ibid.), but this caution really vaccinates the reader against the charge of undue "prejudice" on Hannay's (or Buchan's) part, while surreptitiously guiding our reading of the text. (We are indeed being instructed to "Look at the Irish!") In fact, to a great extent Macgillivray's bigoted grouse rehearses in little the skeleton of Buchan's plot. In his characterization of the villainous (but in the case of Dominick superlatively charming) Medinas Buchan thus shows us both sides of the propagandistic medal: behind the quaint signifiers of a mythologized Ireland—peat smoke, traditional crafts (symbolized by the spinning wheel), an oral tradition ("forgotten poetry"), the Gaelic language—lurks, the novel warns, a rebellious, homicidal race, represented by not only the Machiavellian Medinas but also the swarms of what the novel terms at one point "the sullen murderous hobbledehoys in Ireland" (ibid., 24). To succumb to the beguiling mental pictures offered by the propagandists of Ireland is, Buchan suggests, precisely to lose all sense of history, both ancient and recent: a condition symbolized by the loss of memory which is the primary effect of Medina's hypnotic powers[25]—the three hostages (all from the upper classes), like the others he mesmerizes, become blank slates without any knowledge of the past; thus robbed of memory they become quiescent zombies—precisely Buchan's fear for Britain's governing classes. In Medina's attempts to make a "dog" (ibid., 110), a "satellite" (ibid., 249), a "slave" (ibid., 132) of Hannay, one can trace the outlines of a paranoid fantasy of Britain's own, newly independent "satellite" turning against its former master. In *The Three Hostages,* then, one encounters a variant of that familiar narrative template, the tale of reverse colonization, but with a difference: instead of conventional invasion, a war over territory (the paradigm of the genre from Chesney's *The Battle of Dorking* to *The War of the Worlds*),[26] one finds a campaign of recoding, directed against the centers of imperial power.

But the novel not only serves as an aggressive counterblast to Ireland's putative campaign of propagandistic bewitchment during the period that saw the birth of the Free State. More broadly, Buchan invokes growing anxieties of a general crisis of imperial dissolution or disintegration, one similarly bound up with issues of information control. Strikingly, Buchan takes pains to establish Medina as a blended figure, not only an embodiment of a hostile Ireland but also a kind of overdetermined representation of the wider colonial world. Again, to all appearance Medina appears to be the consummate Englishman, with just a touch of assimilable foreignness ("He is," one character says, "as exotic as the young Disraeli and as English as the late Duke of Devonshire" [ibid., 57]). But a little scratching beneath the surface reveals him as not only a dangerously unbalanced Hibernian, but one deeply immersed in "Indian magic" (ibid., 87), and possessed moreover of anatomical features which the ex-colonial Hannay cannot help associating with a black African physiognomy: "The way he brushed his hair front and back made it [his head] look square, but I saw that it was really round, the roundest head I have ever seen except in a Kaffir" (ibid., 53–54). (Perhaps it is this "hideous roundness of his head" [ibid., 252] which prompts him to spit in Hannay's face, since this is in the hero's estimation "a filthy Kaffir trick" [ibid., 110].)

Ireland, India, and even Africa thus unite in the figure of Medina, though the first two connections are the more salient here: Medina lusts for "a true marriage of East and West," a union whose "seed will rule the world" (ibid., 119). To this end, he has formed a league with the "oriental necromancer" (ibid., 122) Kharama, another master of thought control, whose arts constitute the Indian counterpart to Irish magic.[27] It is difficult not to suspect that Buchan intended his readers to draw connections between his fictional Indian spellbinder and Gandhi, about whose putative derangement of mind he has his collection of Thursday Club elites speculate over dinner ("We would have drifted into politics, if Pugh had not asked [Sandy] his opinion of Gandhi. That led him into an exposition of the meaning of the fanatic, a subject on which he was well qualified to speak, for he had consorted with most varieties" [ibid., 63]). Kharama, like Gandhi (from Buchan's perspective), is a dangerously charismatic figure from the East (his very name suggests "charisma"), who negotiates easily the cultural borderlines between East and West (in one scene he appears in evening dress, later discarded in favor of "flowing robes" which permit a disgusted Hannay a glimpse of his "beastly bare feet" [ibid., 171]), and seeks to destabilize British systems of imperial hegemony.[28] Certainly Satyagraha, the concept used by Gandhi both to organize Indian resistance and to transform British public opinion, might well have seemed to Buchan a kind of spiritual weapon akin to the telepathic, mind-shaping powers possessed by Kharama. But whether or not this particular identification is intended, in the context of the times the prospect of a union between separate colonial spheres—here figured as a partnership between Irish and Indian masters of thought control—would have struck chords of anxiety in contemporary readers.

While, then, in the novels I discuss above, the greatest threat to British hegemony which Buchan can imagine inheres in the (in-)formation of shapeless "others"—colonial natives, the Islamic world, the British working classes—by foreign agents, here it is elites and policy-makers at the heart of the imperial system, figures of consequence like Hannay, who are targeted for reinscription by an alliance of colonials and postcolonials. In the real world, of course, this translates to a warning: swayed by the anti-imperialist narratives in wide circulation after the war, Britons might themselves do what their erstwhile antagonists had failed to accomplish, namely, permit their network of colonial possessions to melt away, like so many castles of sand.

So far I have focused primarily on Buchan's multifarious rogue's gallery of *villains* in arguing for the centrality of information to his vision of imperial systems. I'd like to conclude by suggesting that the significance of the Buchan *hero*—certainly as represented by the figure of Richard Hannay—may also be illuminated by this kind of reading. To do this one might begin by asking: What kind of a hero *is* Hannay, exactly? That is, in what outstanding quality or qualities, precisely, does his heroism inhere? After all, Hannay himself deprecates his own abilities whenever given the opportunity: he is perennially, and quite honestly, perplexed at his superiors' insistence that he is the man for the job; in *Greenmantle* he says to Bullivant, "You've picked about the most useless man on earth" (13), while in *The Three Hostages* he tells Macgillivray:

> [Y]ou've got fifty of the quickest brains in Britain working at the job. . . . They're trained to the work and I'm not. What on earth would be the use of an amateur like me butting in? I wouldn't be half as good as any one of the fifty. I'm not an expert, I'm not quick-witted, I'm a slow, patient fellow, and this job, as you admit, is one that has to be done against time. If you think it over, you'll see that it's sheer nonsense, my dear chap. (29)

Such protestations contain a grain of false modesty—but, I would argue, not much more than that. For in fact Hannay's talents do lie in other directions than these, being at bottom, I want to argue (if I may put it this way), metaphysical rather than agonistic in nature.[29]

If this distinction is to become clearer, one must first consider just what kind of "jobs" Buchan's hero is asked to take on in these texts. In every case, they are best characterized as attempts to impose order upon disorder. Whether, in other words, Hannay is presented with the deliberately jumbled nonsense of some inscrutable cipher, with the potential dissolution of the Empire at stake, or put to work in a postwar London that seems to be racing downhill at full speed towards a state of primal chaos, all of his missions can be boiled down to a momentous confrontation with disorder itself. This is made especially apparent in *The Three Hostages,* where European civilization as a whole is threatened with the prospect of total disintegration. The peripatetic Dr. Greenslade, giving the Hannays his professional opinion of the effects of the war on the collective consciousness of Europe ("I hardly meet a soul who hasn't got some slight kink in his brain as a consequence of the last seven years" [Buchan, *Three Hostages,* 12]), warns:

> The barriers between the conscious and the subconscious have always been pretty stiff in the average man. But now with the general loosening of screws they are growing shaky and the two worlds are getting mixed. It is like two separate tanks of fluid where the containing wall has worn into holes, and one is percolating into the other. The result is confusion, and, if the fluids are of a certain character, explosions. (ibid., 14)

And the situation in the East is even more alarming: "Europe is confused enough, but Asia is ancient Chaos" (ibid., 11). Ultimately, indeed, Hannay's adversary is always "Chaos," the restoration of an ordered world his primary task.

Of course, much the same thing can be (and has often been) said about the sleuth—amateur or professional—in the classic mystery novel, whose act of detection, by bringing punishment to the malefactor, restores order to a microcosm of society that has been thrown temporarily out of balance. But the case of Hannay, instrument of imperial order, is very different. Again, it is on the face of it far from clear what special talent or ability marks him as a hero figure at all (certainly not the sheer ratiocinative power of a Sherlock Holmes or an Hercule Poirot). Not only does Hannay come across much of the time as a curiously passive hero (some of his best work is done lying enfeebled by fever in a peasant's cottage, or playing abject lapdog to an abusive nemesis), but it is sometimes unclear to what extent his agency is really necessary to the plot at all, at least as far as the traditional duties of the hero are concerned (foiling the bad guys, getting at the truth, and the like). Even if one considers his chief role to be that of information gatherer, the information he gathers is not infrequently redundant (all of Hannay's reports to Sandy about Kharama in *The Three Hostages* fall into this category, for instance, Sandy secretly *being* Kharama).

In other words, and particularly as the series progresses, characters other than Hannay himself are at least as important as he is to the cause which he serves, with their labors either performed entirely offstage or—more interestingly, I think—subsequently inserted into the narrative by Hannay in an authorial or editorial capacity. In *The Three Hostages* this tendency reaches an extreme: not only Sandy (who with Blenkiron had done so much of the heavy lifting, outside of Hannay's ken, in *Greenmantle* and *Mr Standfast*) but also Hannay's own wife, among others, have, initially without his knowledge, played comparably if not surpassingly crucial roles in bringing about Medina's defeat. Their work is done in episodes interpolated—after the fact, in appropriate sequence—into Hannay's primarily (and at first wholly) first-person narrative. There is thus an interesting pattern in these texts: as the narrative progresses, the ostensible hero tends to wane as protagonist (in the traditional sense), while waxing in proportion as the knowing, organizing subjectivity which in its ultimate form we call an omniscient narrator—the status to which Hannay increasingly seems to approximate or aspire, as it were asymptotically. His chief "action" finally becomes, in effect, the ordering of the narrative itself.

Before venturing an interpretation of this rather odd feature of these texts, I will first introduce another, to which I think it is related. I refer to the presence, in the narrative world of Buchan, of a degree of improbability that, while seriously damaging to the illusion of realism, may provide a clue as to the true function of Hannay in Buchan's fictional universe. Standing in sharp contradistinction to the state of radical "confusion" implied by Greenslade's metaphor (to which I will return in a moment), the diegetic world Buchan's characters inhabit is characterized by a seemingly absolute *lack* of randomness and disorder—a tendency so marked that it is all but fatal to any pretensions to verisimilitude. In other words, while Buchan's novels frequently invoke the dread of civilizational or imperial disintegration (for Buchan, largely the same thing), they *enact* a rather precise inversion, or dogged reversal, of such a process. Brimming with steadily accumulating improbabilities, the Buchan novel depicts a world of which it is only mildly hyperbolic to assert that *nothing at all* is random, contingent, or out of place. It is impossible to offer more than an (entirely representative) example here: When in *Greenmantle* Hannay (coming from England) bumps into his old friend Peter Pienaar (coming from Africa) on the ship he happens to board (in Portugal), his pleased but not at all disconcerted response ("Here was a piece of sheer monumental luck" [35]) may not strike the reader as *unduly* complacent. But when later in the same novel, after they have been separated in Germany, the two meet *again*, against immeasurable odds, at a random spot on the Danube (Hannay drifting past in a supply barge laden with munitions, Pienaar sitting serenely beside a pier), one feels that a stronger reaction than mere, even if strong, "surprise" (109) is called for. But then, the miraculous encounter is par for the course in Buchan[30]—as are dreams that prove prescient, serendipitously accurate guesses about the future, chance remarks that provide crucially necessary information, and a host of other highly improbable events. Even a casual perusal of the Hannay novels will multiply examples indefinitely.

Of course, as Bakhtin reminds us, improbable events—even much the same particular improbable events as these ("Meetings with unexpected friends or enemies . . . fortune-telling, prophecy, prophetic dreams, premonitions and sleeping potions" [*Dialogic Imagination,* 88])—have been indispensible features of the adventure story since antiquity. Buchan himself seems to acknowledge, however, that the modern survival, or revival, of such narrative elements in such luxuriant profusion demands some kind of justification, or at least explanation. For instance, in a prefatory dedication to *Greenmantle* (though the same note might have been appended to any of his other novels with equal aptness), he feels compelled to offer a pre-emptive strike against the anticipated charge of incredible improbability:

> Let no man or woman call its [the novel's] events improbable. The war has driven that word from our vocabulary, and melodrama has become the prosiest realism. Things unimagined before happen daily to our friends by sea and land. The one chance in a thousand is habitually taken, and as often as not succeeds. Coincidence, like some new Briareus, stretches a hundred long arms hourly across the earth. Some day, when the full history [of the war] is written . . . the poor romancer will give up business and fall to reading Miss Austen in a hermitage. (3)

Once more, the war's to blame: here, for somehow recalibrating the aleatory machinery of the universe, turning thousand-to-one odds into an even chance. Given such an ontological premise, Buchan is actually able to frame his apologia, counterintuitively if not perversely, as a *defense* of realism.

But surely he has taken the wrong tack here. Buchan's chronotope of radical improbability ("Coincidence, like some new Briareus, stretches a hundred long arms hourly across the earth" [*Greenmantle,* 3]) is better understood, not as a betrayal (or, for that matter, vindication) of verisimilitude but as another expression of his novels' overarching ethos. The world of the Hannay novels is charged, one might say, with improbability—which is another way of saying that it is charged with information.[31] Moreover—as his superiors instinctively recognize, even if he does not—the catalyzing presence of Hannay's consciousness is in some mysterious way necessary to the revelation of the stringently ordered system that Buchan's characters inhabit. It is significant that Hannay's one distinctive, avowedly exceptional talent lies in a natural predilection for cryptography: as he says in a rare moment of self-praise, he is "rather a swell at codes" (*The Three Hostages*, 215). Just as, by a kind of patient, half-conscious worrying at the many coded messages to be found everywhere in the novels (from ciphered telegrams to the apparent doggerel Medina sends as a taunt), Hannay slowly resolves their nonsense into information—and also as, in his capacity as quasi- (and increasingly) omniscient narrator, he sorts the narrative itself into order—so does his insertion into the field of action signal that the forces of chaos will soon suffer a reverse. Whether it is truer to say that his consciousness *reveals,* or somehow *creates,* an ordered world, it is difficult to know—but Hannay's subjectivity is undoubtedly a necessary ingredient, the *sine qua non.*

Was Buchan familiar with Maxwell's demon, protagonist of the well-known Victorian thought experiment that would figure so prominently in the development—as well as popular exposition—of twentieth-century information science? Certainly he was well acquainted with the physicist's work: in his biography of Augustus, for instance, Buchan uses Maxwell to clarify his own understanding of Roman "libertas": "it might be defined, in Clerk Maxwell's words, as 'an abandonment of wilfulness without extinction of will . . . whereby, instead of being consciously free and really in subjection to unknown laws, it becomes consciously acting by law, and really free from the interference of unrecognized laws'" (*Augustus*, 149).[32] And whether or not he was aware of the fact, the figurative description of the modern mind in a civilization menaced by disorder which Buchan puts into the mouth of Dr. Greenslade is strikingly reminiscent of Maxwell's famous tableau, albeit in reverse: "It is like two separate tanks of fluid where the containing wall has worn into holes, and one is percolating into the other. The result is confusion, and, if the fluids are of a certain character, explosions" (*The Three Hostages*, 14). In Maxwell's imagined scenario, of course, the demon straddles or inhabits a two-chambered container, separated by a controllably porous wall, and appears to cheat the iron laws of thermodynamics by sorting "confusion" into order, in the form of a patient separation of hot and cold gases—or, in some variants, fluids.[33] "The demon," as James Gleick puts it, "replaces chance with purpose. It uses information to reduce entropy" (*The Information*, 276). Much the same could be said of Richard Hannay—the demon, of course, of Buchan's world. An agent of order whose primary weapon is a subjectivity that foils the prospect of imperial chaos by an accumulation of information, Buchan's demon is a new kind of hero for an emergent age of information—which happened also to coincide with the beginning of the end of British global hegemony.

CODA

ം૭

POST-IMPERIAL MEDIA

I began this study of the Victorian and post-Victorian periods by considering a novel published in 2010. I'd like to conclude by looking briefly at another twenty-first-century exercise in a residual or archaic medium—in this case, a 2009 radio drama. *Torchwood: Golden Age* is a radio spinoff of the BBC science fiction TV series *Torchwood* (itself a spinoff, as well as an anagram, of *Doctor Who*). The TV series, and its offshoots in other media, chronicle the adventures of the Torchwood Institute, a secret government division of alien hunters created by Queen Victoria in 1879 (after her own brush with an extraterrestrial lycanthrope while on a trip to Balmoral). The *Golden Age* episode reveals the existence of a "Torchwood India" branch in Delhi (also personally established by the Queen), tasked with "gather[ing] up all the alien artifacts in the Raj: from the yeti-spheres of the Himalaya to a one-eyed yellow idol to the north of Kathmandu" (Goss, *Torchwood*. All quotations are from this audio recording).

The story is set in the present, the backstory in 1924. At that time, the central office, seeing the postcolonial moment on the horizon (and thereby exhibiting rather greater foresight than one expects from a government bureaucracy), sent agents to shutter the colonial branch, fearing that its hoard might one day fall into the hands of the natives (a reenactment of the Mutiny with alien weaponry is obliquely hinted at). Accordingly, in a science-

114

fictional variant of the kind of knowledge transfer anatomized by Thomas Richards, the "alien archive" was transferred to the imperial metropole ("all that lovely alien plunder [was] packed in tea-chests and sent back to the mother country"). One artifact, however, was left behind: a piece of alien technology called a "time store," with the power to arrest the flow of history itself—the ultimate in temporally biased media, from an Innisian perspective. With it, the abandoned colonials have been able to keep the postcolonial Zeitgeist at bay for decades (the British Empire at last shares the fate of Haggard's Kôr: to be transformed from an empire of expansion into one of duration). Inside their "Royal Connaught Club" it is always the high and palmy days of the Raj—or rather, it is a single, perfect day in 1924, and nothing to do but sip G and Ts, play croquet, read Kipling, and make boorish remarks about the natives.

By itself, perhaps, such behavior might merely mark the inmates of this last colonial outpost (a clutch of veddy British clubmen, led by a demented "Duchess") as embarrassing anachronisms. What elevates them to the level of global supermenaces of the Ian Fleming (or John Buchan?) variety is their nefarious scheme of reverse decolonization: the Duchess means to use the alien storage device to enfold the rest of the world within their perfectly preserved pocket of high-imperial spacetime. This plot is to be carried out by means of a seemingly incongruous alliance of past and present, the imperial will of Cecil Rhodes married to the technological ingenuity of Steve Jobs. With the help of their tech-savvy native "go-between" Mahajan, whose family has served the immortal colonials for generations (shades, again, of Haggard's She), the Britons have been ordering the very latest in American wireless technology (the episode opens with the arrival of an anachronistic "steam train" laden with a new delivery "straight from Silicon Valley"). For the past eighty-plus years, the members of the Royal Connaught have been able to preserve their frozen bit of the imperial climax by means of a monstrous energy web which periodically spreads "across Delhi like a fishing net"—a vampiric network which sucks the lifeforce from the natives, literally consuming them to keep this tiny pocket of imperial spacetime alive. To recolonize the entire world, however, will require far more energy. And so, aided by the faithful Mahajan, the Britons erect a cell phone tower, connected to their alien device, to boost the power of the "energy net." As the Duchess exultantly explains, the network will then use the massive influx of native life-energy to "turn back the clock," resurrecting the Empire on a global scale (even if she is, understandably enough for one born around the time of Victoria's Diamond Jubilee, a bit fuzzy on the terminology, calling the transmitter "a wireless . . . a radiogram . . . thing"). Mahajan is equally enthusiastic, having been duped into believing that he is not only serving his masters but also helping to bring "first-class vi-fi [*sic*]" to even Delhi's poorest.

Old tropes, new bottles. Mahajan is, of course, only the latest reincarnation of Kipling's native operator (betrayed by his masters, he switches sides, and uses his IT acumen to help the hero foil the plot, using his cell phone to send a text message to the wireless mast, destroying it and saving the day). And surely the episode relies on some latent awareness of the shared history of colonial and information systems, some half-conscious willingness on the listener's part to entertain the notion that the present-day offspring of Victoria's webs of submarine cable might have the power to raise the Empire, or its uncanny simulacrum, from the dead. To be sure, the threatened revivification of the British Empire is averted. But further questions hang in the air as the episode ends, suggesting that even the Empire's second and presumably final death (it was, as Žižek would say, dead and didn't know it, like Wile E. Coyote running in mid-air) may not put paid to the power (real or perceived) of imperial media in the geopolitical contexts of the twenty-first century. At the conclusion of *Torchwood: Golden Age*, the listener hears a healthy Babel of voices, as the people of Delhi, blissfully ignorant of the grisly fate that was nearly theirs, go about their business. But the listener cannot help asking: Will they ever get their "first-class wi-fi," perhaps through an act of corporate philanthropy? And if they do, would this extension of technological networks somehow represent a new form, or symbol, of (economic, cultural, or technological) imperialism? Then there is the "White Man's Burden" angle: it is surely significant that the embattled colonials look for aid not to Whitehall but to Silicon Valley; is a comment about a putative American neocolonialism or neoimperialism intended? Or one, perhaps, about the transmigration of the imperial spirit into information systems themselves?

Such questions only further attest to the enduring legacy of imperial media in our own time. For while information systems have certainly loomed large in modern works of fiction and film overtly concerned with the imperial past (including such very different works as Salman Rushdie's *Midnight's Children* and Tom McCarthy's *C*, as well as in the counterfactual realities imagined by authors of "steampunk" and other forms of science fiction), they also continue to shape our thinking about the geopolitical systems of the present and future, in ways that are recognizably indebted to the narratives of the past. For this reason alone one might wish to know more about the genealogy of this relationship, both as a fact of history and as an evolving conceptual entity, a sustained interaction between two ideational spaces. As I have tried to demonstrate here, the imaginative space generated at this contact zone was a fertile one for writers of the age of high imperialism, enabling them to frame and engage a host of topics of crucial importance to them. It is no less the case, in my view, that future work in both fields—the study, respectively, of colonialism and technology in the modern age—can only be enriched by looking more closely at their shared history.

NOTES

⤸

INTRODUCTION

1. McCarthy, *C*, book jacket.

2. Indeed, an early episode in which the protagonist's sister, conceptualizing his penis as a telegraph key, transforms it into a fetish object (22), would seem not unfairly emblematic of the novel's own treatment of old media.

3. In his official report, Serge makes sure that the reader does not miss this point:

> Many attacks on communications . . . seem to be carried out in areas of no military import, and with little practical end. The inconvenience caused to the overall machinery of empire by the interruption of the chain of orders between (for example) a country club and its caterers is negligible. From a symbolic point of view, however. . . . (250)

Serge does not finish the last sentence (the latter ellipses are in the original), but he hardly needs to.

4. This is as plausible a candidate as any, perhaps, for a defining moment containing *en germe* the potentialities of our own age—which is only to show, in another way, the abiding presence and relevance today of Victorian and post-Victorian ways of thinking.

5. The telegraph was, of course, well established by the later nineteenth century, by which time the most salient development, as I will show in chapter two, was the spread of the submarine networks. The ear-oriented technologies of the telephone and the phonograph were developed in the 1870s; the eye-oriented technologies associated with cinema, meanwhile, were following a rather precisely parallel path. Wireless emerged in the late nineties, immediately capturing the imagination of the public, as well as writers including Kipling, whose eerie, eponymous tale of the new technology wonderfully evokes its spookier aspects. (For recent discussions of "Wireless" see Beer, "Wireless," as well as Menke, *Telegraphic Realism*.)

6. See Headrick's *Power over Peoples*, *The Tentacles of Progress*, and *The Tools of Empire*.

7. I adapt the idea of "conceptual integration" from Gilles Fauconnier and Mark Turner. See their *The Way We Think*, as well as Turner's *The Literary Mind*. I may here note that

elsewhere in this book my thinking about the relationship between these two symbiotically related systems has been informed, I hope for the most part unobtrusively, by work in this field. At times my analyses of particular texts invoke the tools and vocabulary of this theoretical tradition; more broadly, I have found it productive, in conceptualizing my project as a whole, to think in terms of a sustained, creative encounter or interchange, at the cultural level, between two ideational fields.

8. Menke writes of "Victorian studies' turn to media" in the years straddling the turn of the twenty-first century (*Telegraphic Realism*, 255).

9. See Otis, *Networking*; Kreilkamp, "A Voice Without a Body"; Picker, *Victorian Soundscapes*; Menke, *Telegraphic Realism*. (For a study of cultural responses to communications technology during the Modernist period, see Goble, *Beautiful Circuits*.)

10. Menke's indispensable *Telegraphic Realism* is a salient case in point, reserving as it does its most substantive engagement with empire for the final two pages of its "Coda," in the brief discussion of *Cranford* that closes the book. Another important study (by Nicholas Daly) of the "sometimes literal" (Daly, *Literature, Technology, and Modernity*, i) collision of literature and technology in the modern age, while focusing primarily on the (British and American) domestic fronts, makes a stimulating detour into the colonial world, devoting a chapter to a reading of Kipling's "Mrs Bathurst," which convincingly argues for the existence of "a special resonance" (ibid., 60) between the Boer War and the cinematograph at the turn of the twentieth century. Then, too, there is *Dracula:* famously adduced by Stephen Arata (in 1990) as a particularly striking example of late-Victorian fears of "reverse colonization," and discussed for its treatment of media by Jennifer Wicke (in 1992), Bram Stoker's 1897 novel has since been subject to analyses (by Thomas Richards, Laura Otis, and Chris Keep) which combine in various ways these two thematic foci. I do not discuss the novel in depth here, both for this reason (it has been much discussed already) and because it is in fact in many respects a somewhat unconventional or unusual representative of the corpus of texts I want to explore here, which are in the main set in, or in any event more unequivocally concerned with, Britain's actual colonial possessions.

11. This formulation, adopted from a phrase by communications scholar James Carey, becomes a keynote in work by figures like Otis and Menke: "If the telegraph became a thing for the Victorians to think with, one of the main topics they used it to think about was thinking itself" (Menke, *Telegraphic Realism*, 135).

12. Haggard wrote in his journal: "I commented on the fact that he had wide fame and was known as 'the great Mr. Kipling,' which should be a consolation to him. He thrust the idea away with a gesture of disgust. 'What is it worth—what *is* it all worth?' he answered. Moreover he went on to show that anything any of us did *well* was no credit to us: that it came from somewhere else: 'We are only telephone wires.' As example he instanced (I think) 'Recessional' in his own case and *She* in mine. 'You didn't write *She* you know,' he said, 'something wrote it through you!' or some such words" (Green, *Rudyard Kipling*, 10).

CHAPTER ONE

1. *Mangal Pandey (The Rising)*, 2005.

2. Albeit with the inclusion of a nauseating scene featuring vats of rendered fat meant to provide ocular proof of a defilement traditionally contested in British accounts.

3. Sir John Kaye and Colonel Malleson, *History of the Indian Mutiny of 1857–8*, a text to which I shall return.

4. It is, of course, as evidence of this durability rather than as an "authentic" example that I have chosen a twenty-first-century movie to introduce this Victorian trope—real Victorian examples will follow in due course.

5. See Gould's discussion of the poem (*The Mismeasure of Man*, 148).

6. In a passage whose penchant for hyperbolic antithesis would not have disgraced Macaulay himself, Seeley asserts: "The colonies and India are in opposite extremes. Whatever political maxims are most applicable to the one, are most inapplicable to the other. In the colonies everything is brand-new. There you have the most progressive race put in the circumstances most favorable to progress. There you have no past and an unbounded future. Government and institutions are all ultra-English. All is liberty, industry, invention, innovation, and as yet tranquility. Now if this alone were Greater Britain, it would be homogeneous, all of a piece; and, vast and boundless as the territory is, we might come to understand its affairs. But there is at the same time another Greater Britain, surpassing this in population though not in territory, and it is everything which this is not. India is all past and, I may almost say, has no future" (Seeley, *The Expansion of England*, 204).

7. A contemporary history of the laying of the transatlantic cable is Field's *History of the Atlantic Telegraph to the Return of the Expedition of 1865*. For a recent, popular history see Gordon's *A Thread Across the Ocean*.

8. Most of the information about O'Shaughnessy and the early history of the telegraph in India presented here is derived from the contemporary accounts cited elsewhere in this section (Highton, *The Electric Telegraph*; Turnbull, *The Electro-Magnetic Telegraph*; the *Quarterly Review*). For a recent account of this history see Gorman, "Sir William O'Shaughnessy, Lord Dalhousie, and the Establishment of the Telegraph System in India," 581–601.

9. In her *Children's History of India*, M. B. Synge depicts Dalhousie as a hero-martyr perishing virtually in the act of reterritorializing India by the construction of communications networks: "A colossal worker, he sought to bind together the scattered parts by telegraph and railway" as well as canal, dying soon after "when his physical strength failed to bear the burden" (quoted in Carter and Harlow, *Archives of Empire*, 548).

10. The blood-colored jacket of the first American edition, upon which a red-turbaned Indian glares with red-eyed menace, gives a fair indication of the writing within.

11. "The film is a textbook example of the Lacanian thesis on how the subject's truth is constituted by the discourse of the Other: the narratrice gradually puts all the pieces together and (re)constructs the events, realizing that she was unknowingly the central piece of an intricate plot—in short, she finds her truth outside herself, in the intersubjective network whose effects elude her grasp" (Žižek, *Enjoy Your Symptom!*, 151–52).

12. "What, then, is the Matrix? Simply what Lacan called the 'big Other,' the virtual symbolic order, the network that structures reality for us. This dimension of the 'big Other' is that of the constitutive *alienation* of the subject in the symbolic order: the big Other pulls the strings; the subject doesn't speak, he 'is spoken' by the symbolic structure" (Žižek, *The Parallax View*, 312). The quotation also appears, virtually verbatim, in Žižek's essay "*The Matrix*: Or, the Two Sides of Perversion," in The Matrix and Philosophy, 244.

13. While we have all read strained attempts to force literary texts to fit into such paradigms, I must confess that the treatment of the Indian network in nineteenth-century British accounts may be one of those cases leading one grudgingly to suspect that the Lacanians might be on to something.

14. Sir Charles Crosthwaite's phrase, made the title of Jan Morris's chapter on the rebellion in *Heaven's Command: An Imperial Progress* (218–248).

15. Tracy, for his part, hedges his own bets in a footnote: "This statement is made on the

authority of Holmes's 'History of the Indian Mutiny,' Cave-Browne's 'The Punjab & Delhi,' and 'The Punjab Mutiny Report,' though it is claimed that William Brendish, who is still living, was on duty at the Delhi Telegraph Office throughout the night of May 10th" (Tracy, *The Red Year,* 46).

16. An event Rujub had unwittingly foretold by calling forth a kind of cinematic, magic-lantern vision during his act.

17. A scenario rather reminiscent of the vampire hunters' use of Mina in the roughly contemporaneous *Dracula,* a novel which (again) Chris Keep, Laura Otis, and Jennifer Wicke have all considered in relation to developments in information technology.

18. An interesting anticipation, perhaps, of "All India Radio," the telepathic corps forming the central conceit of Salman Rushdie's *Midnight's Children.*

19. See Sussman, *Victorians and the Machine,* 194–227.

20. Insofar as my reading of Kipling's fiction suggests its profound inflection by the Mutiny, it must also acknowledge that his "engagement," in Don Randall's words, "with the emotionally fraught issues of the Mutiny topic is, for the most part, oblique, allusive, and allegorical" (Randall, "Post-Mutiny Allegories of Empire," 98). In his essay on *The Jungle Books,* in which he discerns "post-Mutiny allegories of empire," Randall writes: "Unlike so many of his predecessors and contemporaries—Meadows Taylor, G. A. Henty, Flora Annie Steel, among others—Kipling never produced what one might properly call 'a mutiny tale.' Given, however, Kipling's status as the popularly acclaimed 'bard' of the Indian empire, his silence upon the topic seems strange indeed. . . . Making an abundantly documented case, [Patrick Brantlinger] establishes the 1857 revolt as an emotionally charged, key referent of later-nineteenth-century imperial mythmaking and ideology. To accept, then, the main thrust of Brantlinger's argument is to recognize that the Mutiny constitutes, for Kipling, an *unavoidable* topic. The question is not *if* but rather *where* and *how* he addressed it" (ibid., 97).

21. Another figure that might be mentioned here, though no willing servant of Empire, is the leprous "Silver Man" from "The Mark of the Beast." The formless, or half-formed, body of this uncanny "creature" is incapable of articulate speech or determinate gesture; nonetheless it positively radiates inchoate and vaguely meaningful expression. Strictly speaking, the leper is of course "de-formed" by disease, but the figure is depicted as more "pre-formed," embryonic; one is reminded of the etymological provenance of "information," precisely the quantity that his shapeless body cannot produce. The Indian emanates only repeated, cryptic "mewings"; similarly, his body transmits nonverbal, wavelike signals rather recalling Kristeva's "pulsions": "though the Silver Man had no face, you could see horrible feelings passing through the slab that took its place, exactly as waves of heat play across red-hot iron—gun-barrels for instance" (Kipling, *Life's Handicap,* 188), this last phrase referring to the hastily improvised inquisition the protagonists assemble in order to force speech from the figure. But utterance, when it comes, like the unnameable tortures the Englishmen inflict, literally cannot be represented. His subsequent hieratic gesture, however, proves efficacious as a performative, as the victim of his curse is cured. The tale thus provides a horrible but eloquent image of the Indian as an uncanny and presymbolic signifying body, the agent of a grotesquely somatic (infantile or bestial) semiosis enjoined (here, at heated gunpoint) to produce information.

22. During a recent Google search for "Macaulay" and "Indian" I inadvertently typed "f" instead of "d" and was immediately prompted to click on the phrase "macaulay's [*sic*] infamous statement"—which, out of curiosity, I did, only to learn that there is still some disagreement about *which* statement in the Minute this phrase should refer to.

23. In the article version of Homi Bhabha's "Of Mimicry and Man," later incorporated into *The Location of Culture*, "infamous" is actually made part of the *title* of Macaulay's Minute, through a (Freudian?) typographic error: "The absurd extravagance of Macaulay's *Infamous Minute* (1835) . . . [etc.]" (Bhabha, "Of Mimicry and Man," 127).

24. I adopt here the mode of expression characteristic of conceptual metaphor theory. See Lakoff and Johnson, *Metaphors We Live By*.

25. It is his aged gull's ignorance of "the lightning-post" (Kipling, *Plain Tales from the Hills*, 114) that assures the deception's lasting success. Sylvia Pamboukian discusses the deceptive use of the telegraph in this story in considering the theme of science and fraudulence in Kipling, arguing that "[i]n Kipling's stories, modern technologies, such as the automobile and the telegraph, both act as conduits for supernatural phenomena and participate in frauds which fool gullible bystanders into believing in the supernatural. For example, in 'The Dreitarbund' (1887) and 'In the House of Suddhoo' (1886), women and Indians are conned by the skillful use of the telegraph into believing that another person has magical abilities. Conversely, in 'By Word of Mouth' (1887), a telegraph may have been used to carry a message from beyond the grave. In 'Wireless' (1902) an experimental radio may have been magically co-opted by poetic spirits trying to communicate with a like-minded scientist. While in the former two stories women and Indians are gullible figures, easily manipulated by charlatans who exploit the telegraph's potential, the white men in the latter two stories are equally confused by the telegraph and the radio, as are we as readers. We are unable to distinguish between deception, coincidence and legitimate supernatural phenomena. Taken together, these stories probe the nature of gullibility in the modern world: they ask whether gullibility is inherently a part of the modern condition since technology diminishes our ability to distinguish confidently between the legitimate and the fraudulent" (Pamboukian, "Science, Magic and Fraud in the Short Stories of Rudyard Kipling," 430).

26. It is tempting, indeed, to consider the youthful episode as a kind of primal scene or formative event in Kipling's career, one which may have contributed to the proliferation in his work of the Indian information worker—a symptomatic figure, perhaps, whose obsessive replication may have been a kind of imaginative attempt to exorcise the anxiety-making specter of posthuman union with the native.

27. The telegraph influenced Hemingway in his drive to "pare his prose to the bone" (Carey, *Communication as Culture*, 14). (Of course, Kipling's own narrative voice could demonstrate a similar plainness.)

28. That "telegraphese" might be the natural language of power is implied by a minor Kipling poem, which argues that power may inhere in the unspoken, or at least that the language of the dominant tends towards the radically laconic. Contrasting the linguistic predilections, and putatively the essential natures, of "the Celt" and "the English," Kipling concludes, referring to the latter: "In telegraphic sentences, half swallowed at the ends, / They hint a matter's inwardness—and there the matter ends. / And while the Celt is talking from Valencia to Kirkwall, / The English—ah, the English!—don't say anything at all!" (Kipling, *Actions and Reactions*, 240).

CHAPTER TWO

1. In his *Telegraphic Realism*, Menke also invokes Bakhtin, proposing to read the telegraph "as a *chronotope* for realist fiction" itself (95, emphasis original), aligning the technology, and its associations of boundless connectivity, with the generic ambitions of writers

like George Eliot, Charles Dickens, and Henry James. But other chronotopes could be discerned or constructed from the media ecologies of the nineteenth century. If the connective wire could figure the mimetic project of the realist novel, a range of media, I want to show, helped to underpin later-Victorian figurations of an imperial system whose rapid growth and evolution presented significant problems of collective conceptualization.

2. "[S]ome of the most spectacular engineering triumphs of the Victorians, most notably the ocean-traversing steamship and especially the submarine telegraph, precipitated a fundamental restructuring of imperial political thought" (Bell, *The Idea of Greater Britain*, 526).

3. The idea, as Bell puts it, "that the world had shrunk to a manageable size" (ibid., 528).

4. Useful studies of Innis and his work include Carey, "Harold Adams Innis and Marshall McLuhan"; Czitrom, *Media and the American Mind*; and Watson, *Marginal Man*. The influence of Innis on modern thought is greater than his relative obscurity might indicate, largely owing to his influence on McLuhan.

5. A brief rehearsal of the Mahdist rebellion, which I believe constitutes one important subtext within Corelli's novel especially, may be helpful: In the early 1880s Muhammad Ahmad, a holy man calling himself the Mahdi ("Expected One" or "Guided One"), defied the British power in Egypt at the head of an army of dervishes. After the annihilation of an Egyptian force under General William Hicks in 1883, the popular and charismatic Charles "Chinese" Gordon was sent to Khartoum, ostensibly to supervise the withdrawal of Egyptian forces from the Sudan. Once in place, however, Gordon unilaterally changed course, announcing his intention to resist the Mahdists, who besieged Khartoum in March 1884. In January of the following year the city was taken and Gordon killed, giving rise to widespread grief back home for the Christian "martyr," as well as popular anger directed at the Prime Minister, who was perceived as having callously abandoned Gordon to his fate. Victoria, as outraged as any of her subjects, allowed a "furious telegram" excoriating Gladstone to be transmitted *en clair* (Trench, *The Road to Khartoum*, 293) (see also note 16).

6. I have especially in mind "the familiar textbook triumvirate of mid-Victorian imperialist ideology" (John Gross's phrase, quoted in Wormell, *Sir John Seeley and the Uses of History*, 97): Seeley's *The Expansion of England*, discussed above (1882); James Anthony Froude's *Oceana: or England and Her Colonies* (1886); and Sir Charles Dilke's *Problems of Greater Britain* (1890).

7. Any account of such technologies, particularly the phonograph, must be indebted to the work of Lisa Gitelman, who considers "mechanized inscription as integral . . . to the climate of representation that emerged toward the end of the nineteenth century and has dominated the twentieth" (Gitelman, *Scripts, Grooves, and Writing Machines*, 2). For other important recent work on the phonograph and its cultural impact see John Picker's *Victorian Soundscapes*, as well as Ivan Kreilkamp's essay, "A Voice without a Body: The Phonographic Logic of 'Heart of Darkness.'"

8. On Haggard's relationship to the imperial romance, see Katz, *Rider Haggard and the Fiction of Empire*, and Chrisman, *Rereading the Imperial Romance*.

9. See Galvan, "Christians, Infidels, and Women's Channeling in the Writings of Marie Corelli" and *The Sympathetic Medium*.

10. I am invoking, of course, the Tory inversion of Gladstone's popular sobriquet in the wake of Gordon's demise, with "G[rand] O[ld] M[an]" changed to "M[urderer] O[f] G[ordon]."

11. Corelli's own considerable dislike of Gladstone and his politics was miraculously, if only temporarily, transmuted to grateful adulation by a pair of personal visits ("The Grand Old Man came *again*," she exulted to a friend) (Masters, *Now Barabbas Was a Rotter*, 88).

12. Despite his anti-imperialist principles, of course, in 1882 Gladstone "executed one of the great U-turns of Victorian foreign policy" (Ferguson, *Empire*, 233), occupying Egypt.

13. The phrase is Bernard S. Finn's. See Finn, *Submarine Telegraphy.*

14. Which incidentally makes a hash of the novel's own chronology: Gordon's death is, in effect, exploited as both a past and a future event.

15. As he opines in a letter to a correspondent in Mauritius, the recipient of much daft speculation in a similar vein: "Now here is an interesting point. Our Lord is a man, as a Man He must be in some definite place. Where is He? He rose and ascended from Mt Olives. He descends (Zach. xiv) on Mt Olives. Where is He now? He is in the true Temple above the Altar, just over Jerusalem. You are at Port Louis, I am here, A is at Cape of Good Hope, B is in America. All prayer must pass by and through Him. He is above Jerusalem where Stephen last saw Him, all our prayers ascend by and through Jerusalem as per sketch" (quoted in Trench, *The Road to Khartoum,* 185). Gordon's biographer describes (though unfortunately does not reproduce) the accompanying sketch, as "show[ing] the Temple as a sort of celestial telephone-exchange, with one line going up to heaven, others radiating out to Mauritius, the Cape and the United States" (ibid.). Clearly Corelli's "big idea" did not emerge from a conceptual vacuum.

16. This would certainly be appropriate: from start to finish, the public narrative of Gordon's ordeal in Khartoum unfolded in close relation to information systems, from his obsessive telegraphing ("'Gordon inundates us with telegrams without giving us any satisfactory intelligence,' Wolseley complained") (D. Green, *Three Empires on the Nile,* 188) to his sudden telegraphic isolation (as the Khartoum cable to Cairo was cut by Mahdist forces) and the eventual publication of his telegrams. And his death, again, sent an enraged Victoria to her own private telegraph office, to vent over the web: "Casting grammar and security to the winds, she communicated her fury to Gladstone, Hartington, and Granville in unciphered telegrams, sharing her thoughts with every telegraph operator between the Isle of Wight and their destinations. 'These news from Khartoum are frightful, and to think that all this might have been prevented and many precious lives saved by earlier action is too frightful'" (ibid., 198–99).

17. If there is anything to this identification, the Heliobas novels would also stand in an interestingly contrapuntal relationship to Corelli's satirical *roman à clef The Silver Domino,* in which she would lambaste, among other enemies, the Prime Minister, whom she once again loathed.

18. Aronson, *Victoria and Disraeli.* As Richard Aldous puts it: "[Theirs] was in many ways an attachment of courtly love . . . an intense and powerful friendship" (*The Lion and the Unicorn,* 247–49).

19. See Weintraub, *Disraeli,* 454; Hibbert, *Disraeli,* 314.

20. See Pearson, *Disraeli,* 224, 250.

21. "Disraeli," writes Wohl, "had frequently been represented over the course of his long career as conjurer or wizard and it was an image that indicated considerable admiration for his political tenacity as well as criticism of his want of that most Victorian characteristic, moral earnestness. Now, in the emotional climate of the Eastern Question, the image of wizard was employed to suggest how Christian England had mysteriously come under the influence of a Jew. . . . One explanation was that Disraeli had bewitched the nation and so mesmerized it that normal political values were now suspended" (Wohl, 'Ben JuJu,' 114). Adding that "[t]he images of wizard and conjurer take on a special import for they played on misconceptions of Jewish Kabalistic magic and its supposed obsession with supernatural, occult, and even necromantic practices" (ibid., 114), Wohl cites a number of contemporaneous examples of Disraeli's associations with wizardry:

The Spectator drew its readers' attentions to the Prime Minister, "This great Israelite magician [who] appears and with his wand transforms the whole political horizon." Disraeli has "a half-belief in the cabalistic sorcery, with all its wild spiritual machinery . . . . " (ibid., 114)

In its obituary the *Spectator* argued that he "displayed the genius of a political magician in making English nobles, and English squires, and English merchants prostrate themselves before the image of the policy which he had set up." . . . A letter by Horrocks Cocks, published in the *Nonconformist* (10 April 1878), argued that "the Jewish Premier" in *his* antagonism to Russia was driven as much by Semitic as patriotic urges, for he shared "all the instincts, passions, prejudices, and antipathies of his race," and Cocks continued, just as Esther had conquered at the court of a real emperor, so "Benjamin—but not by *his* beauty—has become a great conjurer in the court of a nominal Empress, Victoria." (ibid., 133)

22. "'You are a Chaldean?' I inquired.
    'Exactly so. I am descended from one of those "wise men of the East" (and, by the way, there were more than three, and they were not all kings), who, being wide awake, happened to notice the birth-star of Christ on the horizon before the rest of the world's inhabitants had so much as rubbed their sleepy eyes. The Chaldeans have been always quick of observation from time immemorial.'" (Corelli, *Romance,* 74)

23. Heliobas is "a man . . . in whose veins runs the blood of the Chaldean kings—earnest and thoughtful Orientals, who were far wiser in their generation perhaps than we, with all our boasted progress, are in ours" (ibid., 221).

24. Niall Ferguson paints a portrait of Victoria at Osbourne, on the Isle of Wight, which strikingly suggests both her eager interest in, and her "virtual" relation to, the empire: "In one of the more obscure corners of Osborne House is a clue to why the Queen felt in closer touch with her Empire as she grew older. It was not considered worthy of preservation when the house was given to the nation in 1902, but downstairs in the Household Wing was the Queen's telegraph office. By the 1870s messages from India could reach here in a matter of hours; and the Queen read them attentively" (Ferguson, *Empire,* 167–68).

25. The epithet used by Jan Morris in *Heaven's Command: An Imperial Progress* (490–513).

26. Viewed as a contribution to the cultural construction and circulation of Victoria's public image, Corelli's fiction must also be considered in the context of what John Plunkett has shown to be a "media making of the monarchy" without historical precedent. As Plunkett (whose study focuses on the period 1837–1870) notes, in the nineteenth century "[t]he royal image was constantly available on a diverse assortment of media, ranging from engravings and magic lantern shows to street ballads and photographs" (Plunkett, *Queen Victoria,* 2–3), with the popular press playing an especially crucial role in "the cultural production of Victoria" (ibid., 7).

27. For a discussion of these and other (often contradictory) accounts of this ancient waterway see Redmount, "The Wadi Tumilat and the 'Canal of the Pharaohs,'" 127–35.

28. "Nearly all the bodies," reports Holly, "so masterly was the art with which they had been treated, were as perfect as on the day of death thousands of years before. Nothing came to injure them in the deep silence of the living rock: they were beyond the reach of heat and cold and damp, and the aromatic drugs with which they had been saturated were evidently practically everlasting in their effect" (Haggard, *She,* 184).

29. As she asks Holly: "[H]ow comest thou to speak Arabic? It is my own dear tongue, for Arabian am I by my birth. . . . Yet dost thou not speak it as we used to speak. Thy talk doth lack the music of the sweet tongue of the tribes of Hamyar which I was wont to hear. Some of the words too seemed changed, even as among these Amahagger, who have debased and defiled its purity, so that I must speak with them in what is to me another tongue" (ibid., 146). And again: "Ah, thou canst speak the Latin tongue, too! It hath a strange ring in my ears after all these days, and it seems to me that thy accent does not fall as the Romans put it" (ibid., 147). Later Holly complains that Ayesha "speak[s] in Greek, which . . . I found . . . rather difficult to follow, chiefly because of the change in the fall of the accent. Ayesha, of course, talked with the accent of her contemporaries, whereas we have only tradition and the modern accent to guide us as to the exact pronunciation . . ." (ibid., 175).

30. Some thirty years later, Haggard wrote a novel, *When the World Shook* (1918), which reads in many respects like a (much-inferior) rehearsal of *She,* and in which cinematography (the medium being well established by this time) explicitly features. In it a trio of Britishers are shipwrecked on an uncharted South Pacific island inhabited by a prototypical Haggard lost race, "a wonderfully handsome people, tall and straight with regularly shaped features and nothing of the negro about them" (Haggard, *When the World Shook*, 65). Also according to authorial formula, in the island's interior the Englishmen discover, and inadvertently rouse from a quarter-million-years' slumber, the last two representatives of a godlike white race. One of the pair of sleepers, the beautiful Lady Yva (loved, as it emerges, by the narrator in another incarnation), proceeds to show the Englishmen scenes from the deep-historical heyday of her imperial people, by means of a "cinematograph show" (ibid., 204), causing the moralizing clergyman Bastin to muse:

> I have heard a great deal of these moving-picture shows which are becoming so popular, but have always avoided attending them because their influence on the young is supposed to be doubtful, and a priest must set a good example to his congregation. Now I see that they can have a distinct educational value, even if it is presented in the form of romance. (ibid., 197)

I mention the later, derivative work because it suggests the existence of a kind of conceptual template in which moving pictures are, in fact, reliably constellated with a more or less fixed set of other narrative elements, particularly the trope of the indefinite preservation of life. Another I would adduce is the gargantuan, subterranean "top" (ibid., 320) which features in the later novel's (world-shaking) climax. Described as a "gigantic wheel of fire" (ibid., 321) radiating phosphorescent, colored light rather than heat, this "monstrous, flaming gyroscope" (ibid., 323) is clearly a reincarnation of the great, flaming wheel of life from *She* (to be discussed presently).

31. "Muybridge and Marey," as Friedrich Kittler calls them, "these twins or Dioscuri who were present at the birth of film" (Kittler, *Optical Media*, 159). For more on their work and its historical and cultural context see: Haas, *Muybridge*; Clegg, *The Man Who Stopped Time*; Solnit, *River of Shadows*; Dagognet, *Etienne-Jules Marey*; Clair and Frizot, *E. J. Marey*.

32. Including Ottomar Anschütz, among others. See Frizot, *Avant le Cinématograph.*

33. The idea that Haggard may have been engaged in a kind of literary co-discovery or -invention of cinema is a notion I myself find intriguing, but it is certainly not a necessary one for my reading: the novelist had, to be sure, a wide range of existing visual media to draw upon at this moment in history.

34. One recent popular account of Muybridge and his work is entitled *The Man Who Stopped Time* (Clegg).

35. For these and other devices see particularly Rossell, *Living Pictures*; Ceram, *Archaeology of the Cinema*; Kittler, *Optical Media*; and Mannoni, *The Great Art of Light and Shadow*.

36. Tom Gunning notes that "[a]n alternative to the myth of cinema's sudden invention at the end of the nineteenth century by certain men of genius has often been to de-historicize cinema entirely, to situate its origins in pre-history, with analogies to cinema found not only in traditional shadow plays, but buried within the depths of humanity's most archaic origins, locating cinema's ancestors in the attempt to capture motion in cave paintings, the succession of images in Egyptian tombs, or in the shadows cast on the walls of Plato's cave" (Introduction, *The Great Art of Light and Shadow*, xxi). Writing essentially at the very moment of film's invention, Haggard already seems to probe ancient history, if not prehistory, in search of avatars of the cinema.

37. The conceit that they are confronted with, or actually inside, a giant optical device is reinforced by lines like this: "I rubbed my eyes, thinking that I was the victim of some hallucination, or that the refraction from the intense light produced an optical delusion" (Haggard, *She*, 292–93).

38. Not that the zoetrope was the only moving-picture machine of the age to which one might look for resemblances to Haggard's primal wheel. Indeed, in his *The Great Art of Light and Shadow: Archaeology of the Cinema*, Laurent Mannoni discusses another popular device from this period which went by the name "Wheel of Life"—a contraption whose slotted, phenakistiscopic discs allowed a kinetic sequence to be projected onto a screen, first developed in 1869 by the Scotsman Thomas Ross. "The Ross Wheel of Life," writes Mannoni, "quickly became one of the most popular parts of a lantern show" (233). (Mannoni's description of the mammoth "Lampadoscope" makes it, too, sound worthy of comparison with Haggard's device: this was a projecting lantern comprising "a large vertical iron wheel which moved by means of an intermittent mechanical system. The assembly must have been fairly enormous" [ibid., 232].) But I am finally interested less in identifying Haggard's ponderous wheel of life with any one, particular optical device than in situating his fiction in the context of an emergent culture of the cinematic.

39. A mere three years later Arthur Machen would out-Haggard Haggard in "The Great God Pan" (1890), a novella culminating in its own femme fatale's rapid slide down the evolutionary ladder: "Then I saw the body descend to the beasts whence it ascended, and that which was on the heights go down to the depths, even to the abyss of all being" (Machen, *Tales of Horror and the Supernatural*, 110–11).

40. His book of photographs, *Animal Locomotion: An Electro-Photographic Investigation of Consecutive Phases of Animal Movements* (1887), the culmination of over a decade of work, appeared at roughly the same time as *She*; further books would appear later, including *Animals in Motion* (1899) and *The Human Figure in Motion* (1901).

41. An adumbration, perhaps, of the shifting sands of Erskine Childers's *Riddle of the Sands* (1915).

42. "[T]hou shalt rule this England," Ayesha blithely informs Leo, waving impatiently aside the horrified response ("But we have a queen already"): "It is naught, it is naught . . . she can be overthrown" (Haggard, *She*, 254–55). Soon after, Holly muses: "In the end she would, I had little doubt, assume absolute rule over the British dominions, and probably over the whole earth, and, though I was sure that she would speedily make ours the most glorious and prosperous empire that the world has ever seen, it would be at the cost of a terrible sacrifice of life" (ibid., 256).

43. See also David, *Rule Britannia*, 157–201.

CHAPTER THREE

1. Wells, *The Outline of History*, I.155. In this case I quote from the original (1920) edition. (Wells later altered the wording.) Subsequent quotations, however, are from the expanded edition of the *Outline* (1922).

2. Wells's analysis here also well illustrates Christopher Bush's claim, in his recent study of Chinese writing systems in the modernist imagination, that any given Western conception of the "ideograph" is really "at once a figure of Chinese writing and a figure of a relationship to China" (Bush, *Ideographic Modernism*, xviii).

3. Although, as the work of Laura Otis has shown, such conceptual cross-mappings were by no means always perceived as paradoxical.

4. Wells's evolving conceptualization of "means of communication"—to use his own designation—was fairly elastic. It could refer, of course, to existing as well as possible technologies of both information exchange and transport—trains as well as telegraphs, airships as well as radios. But one cannot read works like *The Time Machine* and *The First Men in the Moon* without being struck by something of the sense of wildly expanded possibility they exude with respect to the question of what might constitute "means of communication" in the future. The new radio was merely one concrete embodiment of a transformed understanding of the relationship between and among a whole host of natural energies, as the electromagnetic theory of Maxwell, with its postulation of a continuum linking electricity, magnetism, and visible light, as well as other, more mysterious, waveforms, found spectacular realization during this period not only in the experiments of Marconi and others but in Röntgen's similarly well-publicized discovery of X-rays in 1895.

5. For an account of the heliograph's use in the war, see Harris, "Wire at War," n.p.

6. In the latter it was used on both sides: the speaker of Kipling's poem "Chant-Pagan" is an "English Irregular" who describes standing on "Kopje on kop to the sun," watching "Our 'elios winkin' like fun" (Harris, "Wire at War," n.p.).

7. The phrase is Arata's; Asimov calls it simply "poetic justice" (Asimov, "Afterword," 214).

8. A scene vividly rendered in an illustration from the novel's original serialization in *Cosmopolitan*, which depicts a line of Martian tripods towering over parallel lines of demolished railway track, a shattered telegraph pole gripped in the extended pincer of the foremost invader. Thomas Richards writes of the paranoid fantasy of the archive of the other, on display in fiction like Erskine Childers's *The Riddle of the Sands*. Beside this trope one might place the Victorian fantasy of the preternaturally powerful (telepathic or telegraphic) *network* of the other; fears of "native telegraphy," in one form or another, were a commonplace in imperial fiction. To the Martians, of course, the Britons *are* the natives.

9. Later, the narrator's brother, fleeing London (first on bicycle, then on foot, then leading a chaise), watches "two trains running slowly one after the other without signal or order—trains swarming with people" (the figure of the "swarm" is a favorite Wellesian trope, one seldom carrying positive associations). The sense of a lack of "order" is reinforced by the inference that the overcrowded trains "must have filled outside London," since chaos in the metropolis has "rendered the central termini impossible"; the gravely damaged railway network thus suggests nothing so much as a decapitated organism (Wells, *War*, 103).

10. By way of contrast: roughly contemporaneous invasion fiction like Louis Tracy's *The Final War* tended to dwell with pride on the contributions made by subject peoples in India and elsewhere to the salvation of the imperial homeland.

11. Headrick, *Power over Peoples*, 177–225. Headrick writes of the central importance of "steamboat imperialism" in the Scramble for Africa.

12. "The undersea cable," writes Armand Mattelart, "was one of the clearest illustrations of Victorian hegemony" (*Networking*, 11). See, too, the discussion of submarine telegraphy in the previous chapter.

13. Much as Wells's expansionist Martians (or in the later text, Britons) are the paradigmatic embodiment of a space-biased culture, his Selenites are the perfect incarnation of a time-biased one; their emphasis on history and continuity is embodied in their internalized media of storage, mnemonic practices, and oral traditions and mirrored by their definite territorial limits and lack of expansionist ambitions. It is worth noting that a culture with no writing, and privileging oral and mnemonic practices, would surely have had, then as now, associations with non-Western, "traditional" cultures.

14. Many of whom, as Headrick notes, preferred to think in terms of "ocean railways" (the equally space-oriented steamships) when it came to Africa (*The Tentacles of Progress*, 49–50).

15. "And how will the New Republic treat the inferior races? How will it deal with the black? how will it deal with the yellow man? how will it tackle that alleged termite in the woodwork, the Jew?" (Wells, *Anticipations*, 177).

16. Recall the contrasting language used in "The Electric Telegraph" to characterize the (Anglo-American) transatlantic cable and the wire to India, respectively.

17. The referent in the original sentence is realism, but the charge's applicability to media is assumed, precisely for the purpose of the comparison.

CHAPTER FOUR

1. Jeremy Campbell's *Grammatical Man* and Everett M. Rogers's *A History of Communication Study* contain accounts of Shannon's and Wiener's work in the context of WWII; for biographies of Turing and Wiener see *Alan Turing: The Enigma* by Andrew Hodges and *Dark Hero of the Cybernetic Age* by Flo Conway and Jim Siegelman, respectively.

2. For a thorough account of WWI as information war see Kahn, *The Codebreakers*, 266–300.

3. There are in fact three possibilities floated within the story—the chief may be living but absent, living but present, or dead—but Pienaar resolves these into a single, stark either-or: there is a chief living within the kraal or there is not; this is, in essence, a figuration of information reduced to its minimal unit.

4. "[Octavian's] malady," Buchan writes, "seems to have been a nervous stomachic disorder to which he was always subject, and which became acute in times of stress" (*Augustus*, 77). It is difficult not to detect a substantial measure of self-identification in his admiration for the herculean feats performed by "[t]his pallid, dyspeptic young man" (ibid., 78).

5. He brings his "passion for order" and immense "capacity for reconstruction" (ibid., 69) to the task, a substantial part of which involves the creation of networks of communication and transport as well as the planned dissemination of cultural code-systems among the populace.

6. He is "a mixture of Rosebery and Balfour," in the words of biographer Janet Adam Smith, who reads the novel as a *roman à clef* (Smith, *John Buchan*, 136).

7. Displaying a familiar brand of racism-inflected admiration, the intelligence officer Arcoll remarks, "If he had been white he might have been a second Napoleon" (*Prester John*, 77); his recent application of a similar epithet—"a sort of black Napoleon"—to Shaka Zulu

(ibid., 72) serves conceptually to link the two figures, and their threats to the empire, in the reader's mind.

8. In her critique of the "conceptualization . . . [of] information and materiality as distinct entities," N. Katherine Hayles coins the phrase "the Platonic backhand," meaning the mental stratagem by which one first "infer[s] from the world's noisy multiplicity a simplified abstraction," then speciously "constitute[s] the abstraction as the originary form from which the world's multiplicity derives" (Hayles, *How We Became Posthuman*, 12).

9. It was Hitchcock, of course, who popularized the term—soon after filming his version of *The 39 Steps*, based on Buchan's novel.

10. Buchan's best-known character, Hannay was brought into being with the Great War: a former South African mining engineer who emerges as Britain's best, if not only, hope as it faces a succession of dire threats to its imperial hegemony. Hannay protects the integrity, often the very survival, of the empire against villains chiefly German in the thrillers *The Thirty-Nine Steps* (1915), *Greenmantle* (1916), *Mr Standfast* (1919), and *The Three Hostages* (1924), all set during the war and its immediate aftermath. The novelist would bring Hannay back for one final adventure in *The Island of Sheep* (1936).

11. In fact, the Germans mean to deploy their secret weapon in the Middle East, rather than Africa.

12. Buchan in fact refers to it twice: "I'm hanged," says Sandy Arbuthnot, "if I can imagine what card the Germans have got up their sleeve. It might be . . . a jewel like Solomon's necklace in Abyssinia. You never know what will start off a Jehad!" (*Greenmantle*, 26). In her study of "the fiction of intrigue" Yumna Siddiqi also notes this intertextual connection: "These novels suggest that imperial hegemony is threatened by disgruntled colonial subjects who have grand empire-building schemes of their own—in *Prester John*, a pan-African empire, and in *Greenmantle*, a pan-Islamic jihad that can be exploited by imperialist Germany" (*Anxieties of Empire and the Fiction of Intrigue*, 13).

13. In *Mr Standfast*, for instance, Hannay must confiscate a bag of "yellowish powder" which "prove[s] to be full of anthrax germs" (Buchan, *Mr Standfast*, 192–93).

14. Indeed, one can imagine the Barthes of *Système de la Mode* parsing "Greenmantle" into a "syntagmatic" chain along the lines of "tunic-girdle-turban": like Solomon's necklace, a pure string of symbols.

15. The phrase, meaning "[s]ay nothing—especially in circumstances where saying the wrong thing may get you into trouble . . . probably derives from the German word stumm meaning silent." http://www.phrases.org.uk/meanings/215700.html.

16. Later Stumm sneers at him, "I never liked the look of you. You babbled too much, like all your damned Americans" (Buchan, *Greenmantle*, 207).

17. For a discussion of the telegraph-bell see Clayton, "The Voice in the Machine."

18. With which disease he threatens to infect the British laboring classes; in *Mr Standfast* the reader encounters once more the threat of a more or less inchoate mass being shaped by a symbol or meme into a dangerous unity.

19. Or rather, the role of "honourable gentleman" (Buchan, *Mr Standfast*, 268) is, according to Hannay, simply one of the many Ivery has perfected: "He could play all parts well because he could believe in himself in them all" (ibid.).

20. One must however assume that even Blenkiron, though a representative of a democratic nation, does not intend here to open the door to the more radical suggestion that *all* class roles might be performative in nature.

21. Ivery's description of the Railway is an attempt to "scare" (ibid.) Hannay, and it succeeds, causing the captive hero to ruminate obsessively in his solitude: "I saw . . . an inn in

a snowy valley . . . a solitary girl, that smiling devil . . . and then the unknown terror of the Underground Railway" (ibid., 242).

22. Of which Blenkiron, in this respect Ivery's true counterpart, says: "Flies don't settle on it to any considerable extent. It's got a mighty fine mesh, but there's one hole in that mesh, and it's our job to mend it" (ibid., 43). Buchan had established Blenkiron as supplement to Britain's state information system in *Greenmantle* ("But so soon as I crossed the Danube I set about opening up my lines of communication, and I hadn't been two days in this metropolis [Constantinople] before I had got my telephone exchange buzzing" [ibid., 154]). In *Mr Standfast* a good deal of the true war takes place offstage, a battle of secret networks. (Blenkiron tells the defeated Ivery: "I've been watching your Underground Railway for quite a time. I've had my men on the job, and I reckon most of the lines are now closed for repairs. All but the trunk line into France. That I'm keeping open, for soon there's going to be some traffic on it" [Buchan, *Mr Standfast*, 279].)

23. In this latter respect Medina to some extent recalls Laputa, rather than the German agents of the previous Hannay novels.

24. James explicitly links anxieties of imperial fragility with the development of the paranoid trope of world conspiracy to be found in contemporaneous fiction: "The search for a common source for all the problems facing Britain and the empire was reflected in the thrillers of John Buchan and 'Sapper.' Both relied on their audience's willingness to accept a world in which secret intrigues flourished and a handful of determined men could seriously devise schemes to overthrow governments or destabilise whole societies. . . . That the readers of such fiction believed that the basic structure of their country and empire was so brittle suggests a flagging confidence in both" (James, *Rise and Fall*, 374).

25. The multisensory assault on the Medinas' victims—between the two of them they deploy visual, auditory, and even olfactory stimuli—suggests the tremendous power of propaganda campaigns in the media ecologies of the modern age.

26. See I. F. Clarke's *Voices Prophesying War* for a discussion of Chesney and the future-war genre.

27. This connection is made clear in the following exchange between Medina and his mother:

> "Dominick, be careful. I would rather you confined yourself to our old knowledge. I fear these new things from the East."
>
> He laughed. "They are as old as ours—older. And all knowledge is one."
> (Buchan, *Three Hostages*, 113)

28. In the event Kharama, in a rehearsal of the plot of *Greenmantle,* turns out to be Sandy Arbuthnot in disguise, the real magician having died before. But until this eleventh-hour revelation the reader is made to understand the grave threat posed by this figure.

29. Which is not to say that the Hannay novels are entirely devoid of traditionally agonistic scenes: Hannay's boxing match with Stumm comes to mind, as does his showdown with Medina in the Scottish Highlands.

30. I cannot resist mentioning one more such meeting: in *The Three Hostages,* Hannay bumps into the German engineer Gaudian, first introduced in *Greenmantle,* the moment he arrives in an obscure fishing village in Norway: "I could have shouted with amazement," he says, "at the chance which had brought us two together again" (146).

31. I mean to invoke here Claude Shannon's celebrated association of information with the measurement of uncertainty, as expressed in his mathematical theory of communica-

tion. (For an account of the relationship between the two concepts in information science see Von Baeyer, 69–80.)

32. The source is not given in the text, but the quotation can be found in an 1858 letter to Richard Buckley Litchfield, included in the 1882 biography *The Life of James Clerk Maxwell: with a Selection from his Correspondence* (Campbell and Garnett, *The Life of James Clerk Maxwell*, 306).

33. Lord Kelvin, "[l]ecturing to an evening crowd at the Royal Institution," used "tubes of liquid dyed two different colors" (Gleick, *The Information*, 276).

BIBLIOGRAPHY

⟨⑥⟩

Adams, James Truslow. *Empire on the Seven Seas: The British Empire, 1784–1939*. New York: Scribner, 1940.

Aldous, Richard. *The Lion and the Unicorn: Gladstone vs. Disraeli*. New York: Norton, 2006.

Allen, Paul M. Introduction. *A Romance of Two Worlds*. New York, Blauvelt: Rudolf Steiner Publications, 1973.

Al-Rawi, Ahmed. "Buchan the Orientalist: *Greenmantle* and Western Views of the East." *Journal of Colonialism and Colonial History* 10.2 (2009): n.p.

Arata, Stephen. *Fictions of Loss in the Victorian Fin de Siècle*. Cambridge: Cambridge University Press, 1996.

Aronson, Theo. *Victoria and Disraeli: The Making of a Romantic Partnership*. New York: Macmillan, 1978.

Asimov, Isaac. "Afterword." In *The War of the Worlds*. New York: Signet, 1986.

Bakhtin, Mikhail. *The Dialogic Imagination: Four Essays*. Translated by Caryl Emerson and Michael Holquist. Edited by Michael Holquist. Austin: University of Texas Press, 1981.

Barthes, Roland. *Système de la Mode*. In *Œuvres complètes, Tome II (1966–1973)*. Paris: Éditions du Seuil, 1994.

Beardsworth, Sara. *Julia Kristeva: Psychoanalysis and Modernity*. Albany: SUNY Press, 2004.

Beer, Gillian. "'Wireless': Popular Physics, Radio and Modernism." In *Cultural Babbage: Technology, Time and Invention,* edited by Francis Spufford and Jenny Uglow, 149–66. London: Faber and Faber, 1996.

Bell, Duncan. *The Idea of Greater Britain: Empire and the Future of World Order, 1860–1900*. Princeton, NJ: Princeton University Press, 2007.

Benveniste, Emile. "Subjectivity in Language." In *Critical Theory Since 1965*, edited by Hazard Adams and Leroy Searle, 728–733. Tallahassee: Florida State University Press, 1986.

Bhabha, Homi. *The Location of Culture*. London and New York: Routledge, 1994, 2007.

———. "Of Mimicry and Man: The Ambivalence of Colonial Discourse." *October* 28 (Spring 1984): 125–133.

Brendon, Piers. *The Decline and Fall of the British Empire, 1781–1997*. New York: Knopf, 2008.

Briggs, Asa, and Peter Burke. *A Social History of the Media from Gutenberg to the Internet.* Cambridge: Polity, 2002.

Buchan, John. *The African Colony: Studies in the Reconstruction.* Edinburgh and London: William Blackwood and Sons, 1903.

———. *Augustus.* London: Hodder and Stoughton, 1937.

———. *Greenmantle.* Edited by Kate Macdonald. Oxford: Oxford University Press, 1916, 1993.

———. *A History of the Great War.* 4 vols. Boston: Houghton Mifflin / London: Thomas Nelson and Sons, 1922.

———. *The Lodge in the Wilderness.* Edinburgh: Blackwood, 1906.

———. *Mr Standfast.* Edited by William Buchan. Oxford: Oxford University Press, 1919, 1993.

———. *Pilgrim's Way.* Cambridge: Houghton Mifflin, 1940.

———. *Prester John.* Oxford: Oxford University Press, 1910, 1994.

———. *The Thirty-Nine Steps.* London: Penguin, 1915, 1991.

———. *The Three Hostages.* Edited by Karl Miller. Oxford: Oxford University Press, 1924, 1995.

Bush, Christopher. *Ideographic Modernism: China, Writing, Media.* Oxford: Oxford University Press, 2010.

Campbell, Jeremy. *Grammatical Man: Information, Entropy, Language, and Life.* New York: Simon & Schuster, 1982.

Campbell, Lewis, and William Garnett. *The Life of James Clerk Maxwell: With a Selection from His Correspondence and Occasional Writings and a Sketch of His Contributions to Science.* London: Macmillan, 1882.

Carey, James W. *Communication as Culture: Essays on Media and Society.* Boston: Unwin Hyman, 1989.

———. "Harold Adams Innis and Marshall McLuhan." In *McLuhan: Pro & Con,* edited by Raymond Rosenthal. New York: Funk & Wagnalls, 1968.

Carter, Mia, with Barbara Harlow, eds. *Archives of Empire.* Durham, NC: Duke University Press, 2003.

Ceram, C. W. *Archaeology of the Cinema.* New York: Harcourt, Brace, 1965.

Childers, Erskine. *The Riddle of the Sands: A Record of Secret Service.* New York: Dodd, Mead, 1915.

Chrisman, Laura. *Rereading the Imperial Romance: British Imperialism and South African Resistance in Haggard, Schreiner, and Plaatje.* Oxford: Clarendon, 2000.

Clair, Jean, and Michel Frizot. *E. J. Marey. 1830/1904: La Photographie du Mouvement.* Paris: Bellamy et Martet, 1977.

Clarke, I. F. *Voices Prophesying War: Future Wars, 1763–1984.* Oxford: Oxford University Press, 1966, 1992.

Clayton, Jay. *Charles Dickens in Cyberspace: The Afterlife of the Nineteenth Century in Postmodern Culture.* Oxford: Oxford University Press, 2003.

———. "The Voice in the Machine: Hazlitt, Hardy, James." In *Language Machines: Technologies of Literary and Cultural Production,* edited by Jeffrey Masten, Peter Stallybrass, and Nancy J. Vickers, 209–232. New York: Routledge, 1997.

Clegg, Brian. *The Man Who Stopped Time: The Illuminating Story of Eadweard Muybridge—Pioneer Photographer, Father of the Motion Picture, Murderer.* Washington, DC: Joseph Henry Press, 2007.

Conway, Flo, and Jim Siegelman. *Dark Hero of the Information Age: In Search of Norbert Wiener, the Father of Cybernetics.* New York: Basic Books, 2005.

Corelli, Marie. *A Romance of Two Worlds.* New York, Blauvelt: Rudolf Steiner Publications, 1973.

———.*The Silver Domino; or Side Whispers, Social and Literary.* London: Lamley and Co., 1895.

The Cosmopolitan: A Monthly Illustrated Magazine, May 1901.

Czitrom, Daniel. *Media and the American Mind: From Morse to McLuhan.* Chapel Hill: University of North Carolina Press, 1982.

Dagognet, François. *Etienne-Jules Marey: A Passion for the Trace.* Translated by Robert Galeta with Jeanine Herman. New York: Zone Books, 1992.

Daly, Nicholas. *Literature, Technology, and Modernity, 1860–2000.* Cambridge: Cambridge University Press, 2004.

David, Deirdre. *Rule Britannia: Women, Empire, and Victorian Writing.* Ithaca, NY: Cornell University Press, 1995.

Dickson, W. K. L., and Antonia Dickson. *History of the Kinetograph, Kinetoscope and Kinetophonograph.* New York: The Museum of Modern Art, 1895, 2000.

Fauconnier, Gilles, and Mark Turner. *The Way We Think: Conceptual Blending and the Mind's Hidden Complexities.* New York: Basic Books, 2002.

Federico, Annette R. *Idol of Suburbia: Marie Corelli and Late-Victorian Literary Culture.* Charlottesville: University Press of Virginia, 2000.

Ferguson, Niall. *Empire: How Britain Made the Modern World.* London: Penguin, 2004.

Field, Henry M. *History of the Atlantic Telegraph to the Return of the Expedition of 1865.* New York: Scribner, 1866.

Finn, Bernard S. *Submarine Telegraphy: The Grand Victorian Technology.* Margate: Science Museum, 1973.

Frizot, Michel. *Avant le Cinématograph: La Chronophotographie: Temps, Photographie et Mouvement autour de E.-J. Marey.* Dijon: Imprimerio Fuchey S. A., 1984.

Galvan, Jill. "Christians, Infidels, and Women's Channeling in the Writings of Marie Corelli." *Victorian Literature and Culture* 31.1 (2003): 83–97.

———. *The Sympathetic Medium: Feminine Channeling, the Occult, and Communication Technologies, 1859–1919.* Ithaca, NY: Cornell University Press, 2010.

Gitelman, Lisa. *Scripts, Grooves, and Writing Machines: Representing Technology in the Edison Era.* Stanford, CA: Stanford University Press, 1999.

Gleick, James. *The Information: A History, a Theory, a Flood.* New York: Pantheon Books, 2011.

Goble, Mark. *Beautiful Circuits: Modernism and the Mediated Life.* New York: Columbia University Press, 2010.

Gordon, John Steel. *A Thread Across the Ocean: The Heroic Story of the Transatlantic Cable.* New York: Walker, 2002.

Gorman, Mel. "Sir William O'Shaughnessy, Lord Dalhousie, and the Establishment of the Telegraph System in India." *Technology and Culture* 12.4 (Oct. 1971): 581–601.

Goss, James. *Torchwood: Golden Age.* CD. New York: BBC Audiobooks America, 2009.

Gould, Stephen Jay. *The Mismeasure of Man.* New York: Norton, 1996.

Green, Dominic. *Three Empires on the Nile: The Victorian Jihad, 1869–1899.* New York: Free Press, 2007.

Green, Martin. *Dreams of Adventure, Deeds of Empire.* New York: Basic Books, 1979.

Green, Roger Lancelyn, ed. *Rudyard Kipling: The Critical Heritage.* London & New York: Routledge, 1971, 2000.

Gunning, Tom. "Introduction." In *The Great Art of Light and Shadow: Archaeology of the Cinema,* translated by Richard Crangle. Exeter: University of Exeter Press, 2000.

Haas, Robert Bartlett. *Muybridge: Man in Motion*. Berkeley and Los Angeles: University of California Press, 1976.

Haggard, H. Rider. *King Solomon's Mines*. Edited by Dennis Butts. Oxford: Oxford University Press, 1998.

———. *She*. Edited by Daniel Karlin. Oxford: Oxford University Press, 1991.

———. *When the World Shook: Being an Account of the Great Adventure of Bastin, Bickley and Arbuthnot*. London: Cassel and Company, 1919.

Harris, Major J. D. "Wire at War: Signals Communication in the South African War, 1899–1902." *Military History Journal* 11.1 (June 1998): n.p.

Hayles, N. Katherine. *How We Became Posthuman: Virtual Bodies in Cybernetics, Literature, and Informatics*. Chicago, IL: University of Chicago Press, 1999.

Headrick, Daniel R. *Power over Peoples: Technology, Environments, and Western Imperialism, 1400 to the Present*. Princeton, NJ: Princeton University Press, 2010.

———. *The Tentacles of Progress: Technology Transfer in the Age of Imperialism, 1850–1940*. New York: Oxford University Press, 1988.

———. *The Tools of Empire: Technology and European Imperialism in the Nineteenth Century*. New York: Oxford University Press, 1981.

Henty, G. A. *Rujub the Juggler*. Rahway: Mershon, 1901.

Hibbert, Christopher. *Disraeli: The Victorian Dandy Who Became Prime Minister*. New York: Palgrave Macmillan, 2006.

Highton, Edward. *The Electric Telegraph: Its History and Progress*. London: John Weale, 1852.

Himmelfarb, Gertrude. *Victorian Minds: A Study of Intellectuals in Crisis and Ideologies in Transition*. New York: Harper and Row, 1968.

Hodges, Andrew. *Alan Turing: The Enigma*. New York: Simon & Schuster, 1983.

Holmes, T. Rice. *A History of the Indian Mutiny and of the Disturbances Which Accompanied It Among the Civil Population*. London: Macmillan, 1898.

Innis, Harold Adams. *The Bias of Communication*. Toronto: University of Toronto Press, 1951.

———. *Empire and Communications*. Toronto: Dundurn Press, 2007.

James, Lawrence. *The Rise and Fall of the British Empire*. London: Little, Brown, 1994.

Jameson, Fredric. "Beyond the Cave: Demystifying the Ideology of Modernism." *The Bulletin of the Midwest Modern Language Association* 8.1 (Spring 1975): 1–20.

Jones, Alexander. *Historical Sketch of the Electric Telegraph, Including its Rise and Progress in the United States*. New York: Putnam, 1852.

Kahn, David. *The Codebreakers: The Story of Secret Writing*. London: Weidenfeld and Nicolson, 1967.

Katz, Wendy R. *Rider Haggard and the Fiction of Empire: A Critical Study of British Imperial Fiction*. Cambridge: Cambridge University Press, 1987.

Kaye, Sir John and Colonel Malleson. *History of the Indian Mutiny of 1857–8*. New York: Longmans, Green, 1898.

Keep, Christopher. "Technology and Information: Accelerating Developments." In *A Companion to the Victorian Novel*, edited by Patrick Brantlinger and William B. Thesing, 137–54. Malden, MA: Blackwell, 2002.

Kipling, Rudyard. *Actions and Reactions*. New York: Doubleday, 1909.

———. *The Day's Work*. Garden City, NJ: Doubleday, 1934.

———. *Kipling's India: Uncollected Sketches, 1884–88*. Edited by Thomas Pinney. New York: Schocken, 1986.

———. *Life's Handicap*. Oxford: Oxford University Press, 1891, 1987.

———. *The Man Who Would Be King and Other Stories*. Oxford: Oxford University Press, 1999.

———. *The Naulahka: A Story of East and West*. London: Macmillan, 1908.

———. *Plain Tales from the Hills*. Oxford: Oxford University Press, 1888, 2001.

———. *Something of Myself and Other Autobiographical Writings*. Edited by Thomas Pinney. Cambridge: Cambridge University Press, 1990.

Kittler, Friedrich. *Optical Media: Berlin Lectures, 1999*. Translated by Anthony Enns. Cambridge: Polity, 2010.

Knollys, Sir Henry. *Incidents in the Sepoy War, 1857–58, Compiled from the Private Journals of General Sir Hope Grant*. Edinburgh: W. Blackwood, 1873.

Kreilkamp, Ivan. "A Voice Without a Body: The Phonographic Logic of 'Heart of Darkness.'" *Victorian Studies* 40.2 (Winter 1997): 211–44.

Kristeva, Julia. *Desire in Language: A Semiotic Approach to Literature and Art*. New York: Columbia University Press, 1980.

———. *Revolution in Poetic Language*. Translated by Margaret Waller. New York: Columbia University Press, 1984.

Kruse, Juanita, *John Buchan and the Idea of Empire: Popular Literature and Political Ideology*. Lewiston: Edwin Mellen, 1989.

Kucich, John. "Psychoanalytic Historicism: Shadow Discourse and the Gender Politics of Masochism in Ellis, Schreiner, and Haggard." *PMLA* 126.1 (January 2011): 88–106.

Lake, David. Introduction to *The First Men in the Moon*, by Herbert George Wells, xiii–xxvii. New York: Oxford University Press, 1995.

Lakoff, George and Mark Johnson. *Metaphors We Live By*. Chicago, IL: University of Chicago Press, 1980.

Lownie, Andrew. *John Buchan: The Presbyterian Cavalier*. Boston: David R. Godine, 1995, 2003.

Macaulay, Thomas. *Macaulay: Prose and Poetry*. Cambridge, MA: Harvard University Press, 1967.

MacDonald, Kate, ed. *Reassessing John Buchan: Beyond the Thirty-Nine Steps*. London: Pickering & Chatto, 2009.

Machen, Arthur. *Tales of Horror and the Supernatural*. Edited by Philip Van Doren Stern. New York: Knopf, 1948.

Mangal Pandey (The Rising). DVD. Directed by Ketan Mehta. Mumbai: Yash Raj Films, 2005.

Mannoni, Laurent. *The Great Art of Light and Shadow: Archaeology of the Cinema*. Translated by Richard Crangle. Exeter: University of Exeter Press, 2000.

Masten, Jeffrey, Peter Stallybrass, and Nancy Vickers. *Language Machines: Technologies of Literary and Cultural Production*. New York: Routledge, 1997.

Masters, Brian. *Now Barabbas Was a Rotter. The Extraordinary Life of Marie Corelli*. London: Hamish Hamilton, 1978.

Marvin, Carolyn. *When Old Technologies Were New*. Oxford: Oxford University Press, 1988.

Mattelart, Armand. *The Invention of Communication*. Translated by Susan Emanuel. Minneapolis: University of Minnesota Press, 1996.

———. *Networking the World, 1794–2000*. Translated by Liz Carey-Libbrecht and James A. Cohen. Minneapolis: University of Minnesota Press, 2000.

McCarthy, Tom. *C*. London: Jonathan Cape, 2010.

McClintock, Anne. *Imperial Leather: Race, Gender, and Sexuality in the Colonial Contest*. New York: Routledge, 1995.

Menke, Richard. *Telegraphic Realism: Victorian Fiction and Other Information Systems*. Stanford, CA: Stanford University Press, 2008.

Meredith, Martin. *Diamonds, Gold and War.* London and New York: Simon & Schuster, 2007.

Morris, James. *Heaven's Command: An Imperial Progress.* New York and London: Harcourt Brace Jovanovich, 1973.

Otis, Laura. *Networking: Communicating with Bodies and Machines in the Nineteenth Century.* Ann Arbor: University of Michigan Press, 2001.

Pamboukian, Sylvia. "Science, Magic and Fraud in the Short Stories of Rudyard Kipling." *English Literature in Transition, 1880–1920,* 47.4 (2004): 429–45.

Parry, Benita. *Delusions and Discoveries: Studies on India in the British Imagination: 1880–1930.* Berkeley: University of California Press, 1972.

Pearson, Hesketh. *Disraeli: His Life and Personality.* New York: Grosset & Dunlap, 1951.

Picker, John M. *Victorian Soundscapes.* Oxford: Oxford University Press, 2003.

Pinney, Thomas, ed. *The Letters of Rudyard Kipling, Volume 1: 1872–89.* Iowa City: University of Iowa Press, 1990.

Plunkett, John. *Queen Victoria: First Media Monarch.* Oxford: Oxford University Press, 2003.

Prior, Katherine. "Brooke, Sir William O'Shaughnessy (1808–1889)." In *Oxford Dictionary of National Biography,* n.p. Oxford: Oxford University Press, 2004.

"The Electric Telegraph." *Quarterly Review* 95. London: John Murray, 1854.

Randall, Don. "Post-Mutiny Allegories of Empire in Rudyard Kipling's *Jungle Books.*" *Texas Studies in Literature and Language* 40.1 (Spring 1998): 97–120.

Ransom, Teresa. *The Mysterious Miss Marie Corelli: Queen of Victorian Bestsellers.* Phoenix Mill and New York: Sutton Publishing, 1999.

Ray, Philip E. "The Villain in the Spy Novels of John Buchan." *English Literature in Transition, 1880–1920* 24.2 (1981): 81–90.

Redmount, Carol A. "The Wadi Tumilat and the 'Canal of the Pharaohs.'" *Journal of Near Eastern Studies* 54.2 (April 1995): 127–135.

Richards, Thomas. *The Imperial Archive: Knowledge and the Fantasy of Empire.* London: Verso, 1993.

Rogers, Everett M. *A History of Communication Study: A Biographical Approach.* New York: Free Press, 1994.

Rossel, Deac. *Living Pictures: The Origins of the Movies.* Albany: State University of New York Press, 1998.

Rushdie, Salman. *Midnight's Children.* New York: Penguin, 1991.

Sambourne, Edward Linley. "The Rhodes Colossus," in *Punch, or the London Charivari.* Vol. 103 (December 10, 1892): 266.

Sandison, Alan. *The Wheel of Empire: A Study of the Imperial Idea in Some Late Nineteenth and Early Twentieth-Century Fiction.* London: Macmillan, 1967.

Scott, Paul. *The Raj Quartet.* New York: William Murrow and Company, 1976.

Seeley, J. R. *The Expansion of England: Two Courses of Lectures.* Boston: Little, Brown, 1905.

Seife, Charles. *Decoding the Universe: How the New Science of Information is Explaining Everything in the Cosmos, from our Brains to Black Holes.* New York: Viking, 2006.

Siddiqi, Yumna. *Anxieties of Empire and the Fiction of Intrigue.* New York: Columbia University Press, 2008.

Smith, Janet Adam. *John Buchan: A Biography.* Boston: Little, Brown, 1965.

Solnit, Rebecca. *River of Shadows: Eadweard Muybridge and the Technological Wild West.* New York: Viking Penguin, 2003.

Standage, Tom. *The Victorian Internet: The Remarkable Story of the Telegraph and the Nineteenth Century's On-line Pioneers.* New York: Walker & Company, 1998, 2007.

Steel, Flora Annie. *On the Face of the Waters: A Tale of the Mutiny.* New York: Macmillan, 1897.

Sterling, Christopher H., ed. *Military Communications: From Ancient Times to the 21st Century.* Oxford: ABC-CLIO, 2007.

Strachan, Hew. "John Buchan and the First World War: Fact into Fiction." *War in History* 16.3 (2009): 298–324.

Sullivan, Zohreh T. *Narratives of Empire: the Fictions of Rudyard Kipling.* Cambridge: Cambridge University Press, 1993.

Sussman, Herbert L. *Victorians and the Machine: The Literary Response to Technology.* Cambridge, MA: Harvard University Press, 1968.

Thomas, Katie-Louise. "Racial Alliance and Postal Networks in Conan Doyle's 'A Study in Scarlet.'" *Journal of Colonialism and Colonial History* 2.1 (2001), n.p.

Tracy, Louis. *The Final War.* New York: G. P. Putnam's Sons, 1896.

———. *The Red Year: A Story of the Indian Mutiny.* New York: E. J. Clode, 1907.

Trench, Charles Chenevix. *The Road to Khartoum: A Life of General Charles Gordon.* New York: Carroll & Graf, 1989.

Turnbull, Laurence. *The Electro-Magnetic Telegraph.* Philadelphia: A. Hart, 1853.

Turner, Mark. *The Literary Mind: The Origins of Thought and Language.* Oxford: Oxford University Press, 1996.

Vibart, Edward. *The Sepoy Mutiny as Seen by a Subaltern from Delhi to Lucknow.* London: Smith, Elder & Co., 1898.

Virilio, Paul. *Speed and Politics: An Essay on Dromology.* Translated by Mark Polizzotti. New York: Semiotext(e), 1986.

Von Baeyer, Hans Christian. *Information: The New Language of Science.* Cambridge, MA: Harvard University Press, 2003.

Watson, Alexander John. *Marginal Man: The Dark Vision of Harold Innis.* Toronto: University of Toronto Press, 2007.

Weintraub, Stanley. *Disraeli: A Biography.* New York: Penguin, 1993.

———. "John Buchan Reassessed." *ELT* 53.3 (2010): 372–74.

Wells, Herbert George. *Anticipations of the Reaction of Mechanical and Scientific Progress Upon Human Life and Thought.* Mineola, NY: Dover, 1901, 1999.

———. *The First Men in the Moon.* New York: Oxford University Press, 1901, 1995.

———. *The Invisible Man.* London: Penguin Books, 1897, 2005.

———. *The Outline of History: Being a Plain History of Life and Mankind.* 2 vols. New York: Barnes and Noble, 1920, 2004.

———. *The Outline of History: Being a Plain History of Life and Mankind.* New York: Macmillan, 1922.

———. *A Story of the Days to Come,* in *Three Prophetic Novels of H. G. Wells.* New York: Dover, 1897, 1960.

———. *The War of the Worlds.* London: Penguin Books, 1898, 2005.

———. *When the Sleeper Wakes,* in *Three Prophetic Novels of H. G. Wells.* New York: Dover, 1899, 1960.

Wicke, Jennifer. "Vampiric Typewriting: *Dracula* and Its Media." *ELH* 59.2 (Summer 1992): 467–93.

Wilson, A. N. *The Victorians.* New York: Norton, 2003.

Wittenberg, Hermann. "Occult, Empire and Landscape: The Colonial Uncanny in John Buchan's African Writing." *Journal of Colonialism and Colonial History* 7.2 (2006): n.p.

Wohl, Anthony S. "'Ben JuJu': Representations of Disraeli's Jewishness in the Victorian Political Cartoon." *Jewish History* 10.2 (Fall 1996): 89–134.

Wormell, Deborah. *Sir John Seeley and the Uses of History.* Cambridge: Cambridge University Press, 1980.

Žižek, Slavoj. *Enjoy Your Symptom!: Jacques Lacan in Hollywood and Out.* New York and London: Routledge, 1992, 2001.

———. "The Matrix: Or, the Two Sides of Perversion." In The Matrix *and Philosophy,* edited by William Irwin, 240–266. Chicago and La Salle: Open Court, 2002.

———. *The Parallax View.* Cambridge, MA: MIT Press, 2006.

INDEX